Making It

Right

When You Feel

Wronged

Making It
Right
When You Feel
Wronged

Getting Past Unresolved Hurts

Jeff Wickwire

Chosen Books
A Division of Baker Book House Co
Grand Rapids, Michigan 49516

Published by Chosen Books
A division of Baker Book House Company
P.O. Box 6287, Grand Rapids, MI 49516-6287
www.bakerbooks.com

Printed in the United States of America

Library of Congress Cataloging-in-Publication Data
Wickwire, Jeff.
    Making it right when you feel wronged : getting past unresolved hurts / Jeff Wickwire.
        p.   cm.
    Includes bibliographical references.
    ISBN 0-8007-9340-4 (pbk.)
    1. Self-control—Religious aspects—Christianity. 2. Self-control—Biblical teaching. I. Title.
BV4647.S39W53   2004
248.8′6—dc22   2003015384

To my dad.

After 25 years of painful relationship breakdown we were reconciled, thanks to many of the principles found in this book. Dad, you are with Jesus now, and I am so very relieved to have gotten to know you before your going home. I miss our lunches at that little French restaurant, your big, gruffy hand that was like shaking a bear paw, your knowledgeable mind and your infectious laugh. If not for the breakthroughs we made before you left, your homegoing would have been far more difficult to bear. Thanks for teaching me how to throw a baseball almost before I could stand, to read and to think, and to take risks in order to be happy.

Contents

Acknowledgments

Mentors are rare. They arrive like grand and special surprises from heaven and always leave an indelible mark on one's character and life. I have been privileged to have a few. First, I am forever thankful to Pastor Howard Conatser, who taught me how to stand behind a pulpit, have courage in the face of persecution and risk everything in order to allow God to move. Billy Graham, whom I met only once, made me want to reach the world. I do not think I washed my hand for a week after shaking his. Pastor Bob Wilhite lit the flame of prayer in my heart. His own infectious prayer life, along with his dedication to teach others to pray, strongly influenced me in that crucial arena. And, finally, my Greek teacher, Dr. Mal Couch, taught me passion for a subject that I was sure I would not like. Like someone lifting a shade to let light into a dark and dusty room, he enabled the beauty and power of that ancient language to shine into my soul. I have never read the Bible the same since.

To the Hurting Who Just Cannot Get Past It

This is a book written to the hurting, the heart-broken, the disillusioned and the discouraged. It is about how to handle the bite of stinging offenses the Jesus way.

The hurt that brought you to the place in which you now find yourself happened in one of a number of possible ways. Someone you thought was a friend turned out otherwise. A person in whom you greatly believed has disappointed or, even worse, betrayed you. Perhaps a loved one walked out, leaving you shattered and heartbroken. Trusted leadership failed, and you have not known how to handle it. A promotion to which you feel you were entitled went to someone less deserving simply because he or she knew the right person. These are just a few of the many scenarios in which offense can take place.

Now you are bleeding. You have a dull sense of robotically going through the motions at home, at work and even in church, but your heart is not in them. Although most do not see it, you know you are growing spiritually anemic. Yours has become a life walked with a limp. The skip in your step has become a slow trod. Your former zest for living has been quenched by the cold reality of broken promises and failed expectations. You may be angry, resentful, mad at life, mad at God or all of the above. Like a deadly IV drip, cynicism is slowly poisoning your soul.

Listen carefully: If you do not get past the hurt, you will grow old with a bitter, cynical attitude.

But you can get past it, and that is what this book is all about! You can live, love and laugh again! Do you want to be free—really free? I believe you do.

The following pages spring not only from the crucible of my own personal experiences with offense, but also from people whom I have helped through valleys in my pastoral ministry and from the vivid stories of biblical characters. My earnest prayer is that you will be liberated from the prison of an offended heart and move into the exciting future that awaits you in God.

Let's begin the journey!

Part I

The Bite of Offense

Woe to the world because of offenses!

Matthew 18:7

1

The Attack

Like a great, fiery red ball peeking out of the distant horizon, the Indian sunrise was magnificent. I had been visiting a mission work in Visak, India, for about a week when I decided to take an early morning stroll. The view was breathtaking. It felt primal, like going back in time to an ancient place of mystery and intrigue. Breathing deeply, I soaked in the moment.

They saw me before I saw them. Out of my peripheral vision I became aware of movement coming toward me. Turning to look, I saw three wild dogs emerging from behind a mud hut and closing in fast. In a microsecond I summed up the situation. They were about a hundred yards away. All fur and bone, ribs protruding, eyes wild and tongues hanging from the sides of their mouths like limp rags, they were not approaching to say hello. Forget standing there and showing no fear. It would not have mattered.

I turned around and ran as I have never run before. Propelled by pure adrenaline, my feet seemed barely to touch the ground. No one was around to witness the attack or to save me if the dogs reached me. Visions of dying on a deserted Indian road in the worst possible way fueled my legs. My lungs were on fire and felt as if they would burst. I thought of my family, their faces flashing through my mind. My life passed before me in the same way I have heard others describe when faced with life-threatening situations.

These were not normal dogs. They were creatures of the wild, ferocious and starving. I kept running, refusing to sacrifice even a second of time to turn and see how much ground they had gained, fully aware of what they would do if they reached me. It would take only one of them successfully grabbing my pants leg and then . . . *mob mentality*.

"Help me, Jesus!" my mind screamed. My mouth muttered it between gasps for air.

I could hear their paws striking the dirt, and their desperate panting was getting closer. *Run, Jeff. Run for your life!* The ministry compound where I had been staying seemed impossibly far away, like a hazy mirage in the distance.

"Help me, Jesus!" my mind screamed. My mouth muttered it between gasps for air. I could feel myself running down, using up the last of my reserve, *tiring*. I knew how fast they had closed in, and I knew how far I still had to go. Not good. What would I do if I stopped? Fall down and begin to kick? No, the dogs would overwhelm me. *Run until you drop.*

Just when I felt I could not take another step, the strangest thing happened. *Sudden silence.* Finally risking a look behind, I could not make sense of what I saw.

Lined up in a row like lifeless statues, the dogs stared at me with a look that said, "We would if we could, but we can't." Leaning over and placing my hands on my knees in a desperate attempt to catch my breath, I was both puzzled and overwhelmed with relief. What stopped them? What had caused them to come to a screeching halt? It was as if an unseen hand had seized the dogs and held them by the neck.

Lines in the Sand

"Oh, that's easy, brother!" my Indian host said as I later recounted the story. "Those dogs know they can't come on this property. They know their boundaries. This property is off limits to them. You reached the property line and didn't know it, but they did!"

There was an unseen line in the sand—unknown to me, but not to them. Now I understood. Without knowing it, I, too, had crossed a line. Thinking I was just taking a walk, I had gone beyond an unknown place of safety. Crossing into their territory, I had made myself vulnerable to vicious destroyers.

> Life is all about lines in the sand. Wisdom is knowing and respecting the lines.

Life is all about lines in the sand. Wisdom is knowing and respecting those lines.

Offenses—those hurtful, heartbreaking, anger-producing, ego-busting events that leave us hurt and wounded—attack us the same way. Usually we do not see them coming. They do not send notice of their impending arrival and care nothing about timing, emotions, age or social status. We are caught off guard by hurtful words from a friend. Trusted people in whom we invested time and affection betray us. Or fierce winds of unexpected criticism blindside us, leaving us reeling in pain, and offense inflicts its painful bite! "So the sons of men are snared in an evil time, when it falls suddenly upon them" (Ecclesiastes 9:12).

> Destructive forces such as bitterness, anger and unforgiveness lunge from the shadows and go for the jugular of our spiritual lives.

Offenses are often the aftermath of relationships "gone bad." An explosion of temper, a misspoken word, an insensitive action or a deliberate, malicious act can set off a chain reaction that lasts for years if not handled properly. As a result, enemies that never would have had access to us charge forward. Destructive forces such as bitterness, anger and unforgiveness lunge from the shadows and go for the jugular of our spiritual lives.

Like those wild dogs, they have the potential to bring destruction not only to us, but also to those around us. The only way to handle the dogs of offense is to get on the other side of the line—on the side of God's Word. There—and *only there*—we find safety.

The Church Under Attack

Jesus warned that offenses would happen: "Woe to the world because of offenses! For offenses must come" (Matthew 18:7).

His words of warning have proven all too true. Unresolved offenses are rocking today's Church, leaving multiplied thousands disconnected from God and disillusioned with Christianity, while homes and marriages are destroyed in their wake. The devil does not have to do much to wreak havoc in the lives of God's children. We are doing the damage for him by devouring one another via offenses. "But if you bite and devour one another, beware lest you be consumed by one another" (Galatians 5:15).

Many ministers and church leaders I know affirm the reality of this pressing problem. Members either have offended one another or are angry with the leaders. The frustrating, revolving back door is filled with people exiting over offenses. "Lost clergy, increased health costs . . . divided congregations, loss of energy for mission, disgust by members who leave, and some malfeasance by pastors can be traced in large measure to the incivility and abuse now common in congregations," writes G. Lloyd Rediger in his excellent book *Clergy Killers*. He adds, "But conflict among church members has now become so obvious, persistent and painful that we can no longer deny or minimize it."

How Could He Do That?

I have been privileged to plant two churches. The second one required purchasing a building that needed a lot of renovation. It was a fairly major project, so I hired the construction manager of a Christian company to oversee it. He came with good recommendations from people I trusted. One day he visited my office and requested a ten thousand dollar check for sheetrock so that it would be on site once the foundation was ready. My secretary cut him the check. He thanked me, smiled and walked out. I never saw him again.

A few days later the subcontractor came in and said, "Mr. Wickwire, I am going to need a check to order the sheetrock."

At that moment I felt the familiar twisting in my stomach that happens when you know you have been had. "But we already gave a check for ten thousand dollars to the foreman," I replied. The subcontractor then informed me that he had not seen the man for days.

I called his office. They said they did not know where he was. The project had to go on. I could not let this terrible situation sidetrack the work. Frustrated, angry and spent, we issued another check.

> When he heard my voice there was dead silence.

A few weeks later while driving my car on a hot, Texas summer night a friend who had somehow obtained the foreman's private home phone number called my cell phone to give it to me. I quickly pulled over into a vacant parking lot and dialed it. I recall the conversation vividly. When he heard my voice there was dead silence.

"Bob [not his actual name], where's our money?" I asked.

"I don't have it," he said coolly.

Harsh reality hit me in the gut. Swallowing hard, I continued.

"Then where is it?" I responded, not feeling very spiritual.

"It's gone," he said nonchalantly.

"What do you mean 'gone'?"

I could feel my blood beginning to boil. This man was a professed Christian, not some unchurched man who knew nothing about the Word of God. The conversation continued.

"What do you mean 'gone'?" I repeated.

"It's just gone," he replied.

"Are you telling me you *stole* the ten thousand dollars I gave you for the sheetrock?" I was increasingly shocked at the apathetic tone of his voice.

"Yeah, and what are you going to do about it?" he answered.

I was stunned. Who was this? Was this the same man who had stood in my sanctuary and told me he was excited about our new church? My mind reeled. I did not know what to say to him but knew very well what the Scriptures said about vengeance (which we will cover in greater detail in the epilogue). I also knew that a lawsuit would eat up all my time and resources. Somehow the words came out.

"Bob, I'm going to turn you over to God. He saw this. He knows about it. It wasn't my money; it was His. And Bob, He'll handle it." With that I hung up.

In the meantime, the people who had so highly recommended him left the church. And they never offered any apologies, explanations or inquiries about how we were doing—*ever.*

I knew he went to a large, influential church where I felt certain I would get some help, so I phoned his pastor. Again, I was stunned as he gave me a brief, meaningless "sermonette" on forgiveness.

To my knowledge, nothing has ever been done to the man in terms of church discipline. At least no one ever called to tell me otherwise. In the beginning stages of a brand-new church filled with stress and pressure, no one seemed to care that a professing Christian had stolen ten thousand dollars of God's money.

Struggling with the Dogs

Every day I awoke to the memory of what this man had done, his callous, cavalier attitude and the non-response of his pastor. Consequently, the dogs of offense lunged, attacking my mind and heart. Some days I simmered with anger in spite of myself. At other times I felt the gray fog of disillusionment creeping over my soul. It was a daily effort not to be preoccupied with it.

In spite of the man's theft we finished the renovation, and God's blessing was richly with us. I placed the man who stole the money, the pastor who apparently did nothing and the entire ugly scenario into God's hands. There was really nothing else to do except take him to small claims court or initiate legal action.

In the final chapter I will share with you what finally happened to the man and what God taught me through the entire incident. But one thing was certain: The event showed me the necessity of handling offenses the Jesus way.

> The entire event showed me the necessity of handling offenses the Jesus way.

I have learned that offenses can cripple your walk with God, ruin your vision and extinguish your zeal. They can and do open the door to sin, as well as sidetrack you from your calling. In the following chapters we are going to take an honest look at the tragic consequences offenses can cause, the variety of ways the dogs of offense can lunge from the shadows, right and wrong responses to them, and the marvelous blessings that come to the person who responds the Jesus way. If you are on earth you are going to be offended, and that is why you need both the truth and the tools found in these pages!

At this point you may be asking, "Are offenses that big a deal? Does the Bible have much to say about them? Does this really matter to me, my family or my relationship with God?" Offenses and our responses to them matter more than you might realize.

Follow-up Questions

1. Have you been attacked by the dogs of offense?
2. Are you struggling right now with anger, disillusionment or both because of it?
3. How have you handled it? Have you been successful?

I encourage you to take a moment to make a life-changing decision. Decide that *today* is the beginning of the end for your offense. Start by placing it in God's hands.

There Is a "Scandal-On"!

A married couple simply could not get along. Constantly fighting and arguing, they finally decided to communicate in writing. Notes scrawled on sticky pads began to appear everywhere.

"I've gone to the store. Back soon!" one read.

"Getting my nails done. Back by five," another reported.

And so it went. One night the husband, knowing his wife would awaken earlier, left a note asking her to rouse him by seven. The next morning he woke up, looked at the clock and could not believe his eyes. Eight forty-five! He jumped up, looked for her and darted back to the bedroom where a note lay next to his pillow. "Get up. It's seven."

Though humorous, this story illustrates the ridiculous extremes to which offenses can take us. Later, when the clouds of bitterness clear, we realize that we have acted absurdly. Bitterness can make mature adults behave like elementary schoolchildren on the "playground" of life.

Skandalon—What Is It?

When the children of Israel awakened in the wilderness the first morning following their mighty deliverance from Egypt, they saw a strange substance all over the ground. Moses told them it was their new food. Not knowing what it was, they called it *manna*, which means, "What is it?"

When you look at the Greek word *skandalon* you might ask the same question: "What is it?" *Skandalon* translates to "offense" or "stumbling stone." It literally means "a stumbling block, a cause of stumbling, trapstick, to entrap, trip up, to entice to sin." *Vines Dictionary of Old and New Testament Words* tells us that *skandalon* is "anything that arouses prejudice or becomes a hindrance to others, or causes them to fall by the way." The English word *scandal* comes from this Greek word. We might consider the word *skandalon* to signify that there is a "scandal going on" within us.

> Skandalon signifies that there is a "scandal going on" within us.

To the Greek-speaking world, *skandalon* was the part of a trap to which hunters attached bait—hence, the trap or snare itself. The skandalon in a mousetrap, for instance, would be the little metal mechanism on which we place the cheese. It is the trigger that releases the trap, the lure that entices a mouse into the crushing death grip of the metal arm.

When we become offended, a scandal is released inside of us. An offense takes place and we fall by the way, stumble or trip. The trigger is sprung and the trap snaps down upon us with a deadly vice grip on our emotions.

Skandalon applies to anything that causes us to trip or stumble in our faith.

Offenses come in many shapes and sizes (more on this subject in Part 2). It may be an enticement to behave in a way that would lead to moral and spiritual devastation—like a slip into immorality. We most often hear this referred to as a "stumbling block."

Skandalon also can refer to that which causes anger, hurt or vexation. Our relationship with God can be seriously threatened when an offense takes place. *The Complete Word Study Dictionary* notes, "Skandalon always denotes an enticement to conduct which could ruin the person in question."

How the Trap Is Sprung

When I was a boy I was fascinated with wildlife. Birds particularly intrigued me because they were so beautiful and graceful. But the problem was that I could not get near enough to get a good look at them! One day I decided to try something I had seen on television, but I soon learned that not everything you see on TV can be duplicated. I set up a cardboard box in my backyard, propped up the front of it with a stick, tied a string to the stick and then ran it around the side of the house. Next I took a piece of bread, broke it into four parts and placed them in a trail leading up to and underneath the box. Finally I hid around the corner, grabbed the end of the string and waited for an unsuspecting bird to follow the bread under the box. You are probably wondering if it worked. *Nope.* The birds were too smart for me. But the devil uses the same technique by luring us with offenses, and it *does* work. Let me illustrate.

Indignation

The four pieces of bread represent the four stages of an offense. The first piece is the offense itself. Something happens that hurts you, first causing pain and then *indignation.* You cannot believe someone did what he did or said what he said! Anger reaches a boiling point. You just cannot seem to shake it off, sleep it off, talk it off or forget about it. At this point you have a choice to handle it wrongly by biting the bait and remaining offended, or to handle it the way that Jesus taught (much more on "The Jesus Way" in Part 3).

Justification

The second piece of bread is the *justification* of the decision not to forgive. Justifying your disobedience to God always follows unforgiveness. You remind yourself of all the reasons why you should be able to remain mad. *After all, the person was wrong,* you reason to yourself. You did not do it; he did! You have every right, you assume, to harbor a grudge, give the person "the look" when you see him, talk badly about him and keep him on your black list! Justification of unforgiveness is a defining moment in the progress of an offense.

Visualization

The third piece of bread is repetitive *visualization* of the events surrounding the offense. The longer the offense is harbored, the more deeply embedded it becomes. Like hitting the rewind button on a VCR, we replay the drama over and over. It becomes a maddening thing—in fact, torturous. You want it to stop, but it is as if someone else is hitting that button. This is the pattern of all offenses if we follow the bread trail.

Actualization

The fourth and final piece of bread is *actualization.* Webster's defines *actualization* as "to make actual or real, to make realistic." At this point in the game, indignation, justification and visualization have made the offense so real that it consumes you. The bread trail has carried you under the box and into what Scripture calls the *root of bitterness*. After picking up the first three pieces, all that remains is to eat the bread of bitterness.

Trapped

This is the moment Satan has waited for. He pulls the string, springs the trap and the box crashes down on your head.

You are trapped. Like cancer, bitterness begins to eat away at you. The Bible warns about this root. "Looking carefully lest anyone fall short of the grace of God; lest any root of bitterness springing up cause trouble, and by this many become defiled" (Hebrews 12:15).

Unresolved offenses bring many changes. Both the offense and the offender rule you, your relationship with

God is damaged and you say and do things that grieve the Holy Spirit as well as others.

At this point, it is crucial to come to Jesus, the Healer of your heart, for spiritual deliverance! You must start by giving the offense to Him, trusting Him to help you forgive and release it. Only Jesus can take away an offense and restore spiritual health.

This is the moment for which Satan has waited. He pulls the string, springs the trap and the box crashes down on your head.

Remember the cycle:

- First, *indignation* follows the painful offense.
- Then you begin *justification* of your refusal to forgive.
- You experience repeated *visualization* of the events surrounding the offense.
- Finally, *actualization* sets in. The offense becomes so real that it consumes you. The root of bitterness, like a deadly plant, winds its way down into your soul.

Equal Opportunity Destroyers

Jesus used the word *skandalon* often. He talked about our hands and eyes having the potential to make us stumble. In other words, Jesus warned us not to look at or touch anything that could entice us to sin, thereby scandalizing our faith. "If your right eye causes you to sin [stumble], pluck it out and cast it from you" (Matthew 5:29).

And "bad things" are not the only potential stumbling blocks. Those things that God intends for your good also can make you stumble. Let me explain. Most people think of Jesus as a gentle, meek, timid man who was instantly lovable and attractive. This was not always so. He was often a rock of offense! God intentionally placed Jesus in the world to be a "rock of stumbling." "Behold, I lay in Zion a stumbling stone and rock of offense" (Romans 9:33).

Jesus told the chief priests and Pharisees that two options were available to those confronted with His message. "And whoever falls on this stone [the cornerstone, Christ Himself] will be broken; but on whomever it falls, it will grind him to powder" (Matthew 21:44).

Does this sound like a timid man with a timid message? When we hear the Gospel (the claims of Christ accompanied by the command to repent), either we will fall on the stone (Christ Jesus) and be "broken" from our sinful ways, or we will be offended and the stone of judgment will fall and crush us on Judgment Day. Broken or crushed—these are your options when Christ confronts you with His Word.

Jesus' teachings often cause offense because He requires repentance and change. If we refuse to hear Him and become offended by His commands, our refusal will drive us from Him and lead to our ruin. The cornerstone, Jesus Himself, will come on Judgment Day and grind all who have disobeyed Him into powder. If we repent of our sins and in essence fall on Him, our old lives and ways will be broken, yet we will be healed and redeemed. This is a lifelong process. Time and again we are given the choice either to fall on Jesus by choosing His way or to reject His wisdom and suffer the consequences of our foolish choices.

Jesus Offended Even His Own Disciples!

Jesus' teachings even brought offense to His own disciples. After telling them they would have to "eat His flesh" and "drink His blood," they responded by asking, "This is a hard saying; who can understand it?" Jesus replied, "Does this offend [*skandalon*] you?" (John 6:53, 61, NIV). Indeed it did! Yet they did not allow the offense to drive them away from their Lord. They trusted Jesus, overcame the offense and moved forward in their spiritual walk—that is, all but Judas who was ruined by offense and later betrayed Christ because of it. "For Jesus had known from the beginning which of them did not believe and who would betray him" (John 6:64, NIV).

Whenever the Word of God challenges us to the point of offense, our response must be the same as that of the disciples. If the Bible offends you, then something inside has been exposed that needs the divine touch. Offense at the Word of God is a clear signal of the need for inner change.

> Offense at the Word of God is a clear signal of the need for inner change.

Jesus also cautioned His followers against becoming offended over trials and persecutions. He warned of offenses to those who believed His Word, yet failed to put down roots deep enough to withstand the enemy's well-placed attacks. "Afterward, when tribulation or persecution arises for the word's sake, immediately they stumble" (Mark 4:17). As we will see later, this is exactly what took place with Peter and the other disciples.

Jesus went on to teach that the world would always be a place of offenses. "It is impossible that no offenses should come" (Luke 17:1). Yet He issued a stiff warning to those who cause them: "But woe to him through whom they do come! It would be better for him if a millstone were hung around his neck, and he were thrown into the sea, than that he should offend [*skandalon*] one of these little ones" (Luke 17:1–2).

The apostle Paul used the word *skandalon* when discussing the possibility of making a weaker brother stumble in his faith. "It is good neither to eat meat nor drink wine nor do anything by which your brother stumbles or is offended or is made weak" (Romans 14:21).

These examples alone demonstrate that skandalon is a major issue that should be taken seriously by those who profess love for Christ. But how can you tell if you are offended? In the next chapter we will take a look at the warning signs.

Follow-up Questions

1. As you read about the many things that can cause a "scandal" within, did any of them ring a bell?
2. Did you recognize the bread trail? If so, how far have you followed it?
3. Is Christ speaking to you about offenses in your own life?

I encourage you to be courageous enough to assess honestly the impact offenses have had on you. Decide: Is the offense worth what it is stealing from me?

3

Bitterness—The Frankenstein of Unresolved Offense

I once read about a couple who were saying good-bye to dinner guests. Standing on the front porch chatting, one of the guests leaned against a wooden pillar. Suddenly, the entire structure gave way and came crashing down around them. No one was seriously hurt, but the intriguing question remained: How did this happen?

The truth came out the next day. In short order, a specialist found the culprit . . . *termites*. Over time, they had been busily and silently eating away at the wood. The trained eye could see it, but others could not until it was too late.

Offenses are like termites. They hide underneath in the shadows of our hearts, silently chewing away at the

> Offenses are like termites. They hide underneath in the shadows of our hearts, silently chewing away at the fabric of our souls.

fabric of our souls. Undetected, offenses slowly compromise spiritual vitality and ultimately give birth to deadly bitterness. One day the porch falls in. To the shock and surprise of many, a divorce happens, a church splits or a long-term friendship falls apart—and the termites of offense are the unseen culprits.

Hurting People in Hurting Churches

Billy Hornsby, director of Bethany Cell Church Network, wrote in Bethany's newsletter:

> In these days we hear of so many pastors, church members and staff who have been hurt at different times and in different manners by others in the Body of Christ. The degree of damage caused, whether purposely or in ignorance, varies, and recovery depends on the extent of forgiveness given to those who inflicted the wounds. Bitterness and resentment can shipwreck a pure walk in the calling of God, but a humble, submitted heart causes the purifying fire to drive the wounded deeper into Christ.

Hornsby then asks the following questions. You might want to ask them of yourself.

- Are you guilty of harsh words and unjust actions toward other brothers and sisters?
- Have you been the recipient of such abuse?
- Have you set things right with others?

- Are you standing clean and clear before Jesus today?
- Have you overcome the guilt? The bitterness? The pain?

It would not hurt every child of God to answer these questions regularly. Offenses cannot be ignored, taken lightly or accepted flippantly as a "fact of life." Most do not realize the high price of unresolved offenses. The bitterness they spawn spreads to every touch point of life.

Picture an old wooden wagon wheel—the kind that used to be on the stagecoaches in the westerns. The wooden hub was the middle of the wheel, and the rough, wooden spokes went out from it, touching every part of the outer wheel that took all the punishment. Now imagine catching that middle hub on fire. What would happen? Soon all of the wooden spokes would be set ablaze and the entire wheel would collapse. That is just what bitterness does! It sets your heart on fire, which soon reaches out to all the major touch points of life. Eventually everything is affected.

When bitterness puts down its poisonous roots you lose a sense of the Lord's presence and joy. Your mind becomes preoccupied with the offense and, over time, even ruled by it. Hatred and thoughts of revenge creep in like thieves in the night. King Saul became so bitter that he turned dangerous (see 1 Samuel 18–31).

Gary R. Collins writes, "We've all had the experience. Something or somebody makes us angry. A co-worker gets the promotion that we were expecting. Another person starts a rumor or is unfairly critical. Nobody knows what we are thinking because we keep our feelings hidden, but anger flares inside. Sometimes it festers there for days or weeks, and eventually it turns into bitterness" ("When Anger Turns To Bitterness," from the American Association of Christian Counselors web site: www.aacc.net).

Bitterness Under a Microscope

Bitterness is the offspring of prolonged, nurtured offenses. The ancient Greek philosopher Aristotle observed, "Bitter people are hard to reconcile and keep up their anger for a long time because they suppress their animosity." *Webster's New World Dictionary* defines bitterness as "causing or showing sorrow, discomfort or pain; grievous." It goes on to say that bitterness is "characterized by strong feelings of hatred, resentment and cynicism." Its sour fruit include a critical spirit, animosity, a short temper, self-righteousness and a tendency to be argumentative. Bitter people often believe no one understands them and that the world is against them. They spew their offenses at those closest to them, alienating the very ones who might help. This, in turn, reinforces their belief that no one cares. The embittered are left in a lonely and miserable condition.

Words That Cut

The Greek word for bitterness is *pikros* (pick-ros), which means "to cut or to prick." It sounds exactly like what it does. Lashing out in anger and hurt, embittered people cut with razor-like words and actions. Husbands, for instance, are warned against "cutting" their wives with bitter words and actions. Paul writes, "Husbands, love your wives and do not be bitter [*pikros*] toward them" (Colossians 3:19).

These relationship busters build walls of separation and trigger a deadly domino effect that Ephesians 4:31 describes vividly. I have taken the liberty of inserting brief definitions following the key words: "Let all bitterness [harshness and hardness toward others], wrath [sudden rage], anger [a settled, angry disposition], clamor [loud quarreling], and evil speaking [slander designed to hurt someone's reputation] be put away from you, with all malice [desire to injure]."

If the above list were a train, bitterness would be the locomotive and desire to injure another the caboose. Every car in between carries deadly cargo. It is a train from hell that begins with an offense, and it chugs through the lives of those who should know best how to derail it—God's children!

The Warning Signs

Bitterness leaves several telling footprints on our souls. Some were mentioned in chapter 2, but they bear repeating. Does the following list of characteristics describe you or someone you know?

- The inability to hear someone's name or encounter him or her publicly without being flooded with negative emotions.
- Thoughts of revenge, including fantasies of harm coming to the offender.

- Obsessive preoccupation with the events surrounding the offense.
- Conversational obsession—constantly telling anyone who will listen about the offense, ad nauseum.
- A depleted devotional life. Valuable time that was once spent with God withers as spiritual dryness sets in, and the person feels cut off from God.

This list is not exhaustive. It is drawn from my study of biblical figures as well as personal experience. If any of the above describes you, you may have some unresolved offenses to settle. And you have good reason to resolve them! In the next chapter we will look at a few.

Follow-up Questions

1. Have you known someone whose life was ruined over bitterness? If so, what could he or she have done differently?
2. Do you recognize the warning signs of bitterness operating in your home? Your business? Your church?
3. Have "cutting" words been aimed at you lately? Have you spoken any yourself? What is Christ speaking to your heart about this?

I encourage you to make it a goal to root out the root of bitterness wherever you find it.

4

Here's to Your Health

In the Roman gallery of the British Museum stands a long line of marble busts erected on pedestals that bear the name of each. Interestingly, they enable the viewer to study the faces of the Roman emperors who, each for a time, held the world in his grasp.

Two busts of Nero are there, which is particularly intriguing because they reveal a great truth. The earlier bust is less coarse, the brutal element less pronounced. But the latter bust reveals a great change. The marks of cruelty and unbridled passion are clearly evident. "We see in his brutal face, his heavy eye, his sensual lips and thick neck the marks of the beast he had become" *(Encyclopedia of 7700 Illustrations)*. Between the making of the two busts, Nero had murdered his mother, set Rome on fire and burned Christians as human torches to light his garden. Through the years the seeds of hatred and bitterness left their marks.

Bitterness is bad for your health, and forgiveness is good for you. In an article by Marilyn Elias entitled "Holding Grudges Is Hazardous to Health" (*USA Today*, 8/25/99), psychologist Michael McCullough of the National Institute for Healthcare Research stated, "Growing evidence shows that people inclined to forgive others enjoy better mental and physical health than those who hold grudges." He continued, "Unless they're repeatedly excusing someone who's abusive, forgiveness seems to be a positive act for the one doing it."

In a *New York Times* article (11/20/96), Jane E. Brody discussed the destructive power of anger. She said that anger increases the risk of heart attack by triggering "fight or flight" mechanisms, which cause the heart to beat faster, blood pressure to rise, coronary arteries to constrict and blood to get stickier. Other medical research adds chronic anger to a high risk factor list (including cigarette smoking, a high fat diet, etc.) that can lead to early death.

Solomon observed, "A merry heart does good, like medicine, but a broken spirit dries the bones" (Proverbs 17:22). A Hebrew meaning of *broken* is "stricken or wounded." When we are offended our spirits are wounded, and over the long term the wound dries up the life within us. Laughter fades as the vampire of offense sucks away our happiness.

Jail Time

Some of Jesus' strongest words were directed toward offense and the choice not to forgive. In Matthew 18,

He spoke of a man who was forgiven a large debt by his master. Yet the same man refused to forgive his own servant a far lesser debt. The master became angry and said, "Should you not also have had compassion on your fellow servant, just as I had pity on you?" (verse 33). It is easy to see where Jesus was headed.

We may have been hurt, but our offenses cannot compare to the level of grief God suffered on our behalf in giving His only Son to remedy sin. God has forgiven us the equivalent of billions of dollars in sin-debt, so He expects us to be merciful in forgiving thousands.

Christ's strongest words were used to reveal the man's fate. "His master was angry, and delivered him to the torturers until he should pay all that was due to him" (verse 34). There is no way around these chilling verses. Jesus said that those who do not forgive are turned over to tormentors. "So My heavenly Father also will do to you if each of you, from his heart, does not forgive his brother his trespasses" (verse 35).

The phrase *delivered him to the torturers* has always intrigued me. What did Jesus mean? Who are the torturers? R.C.H. Lenski's commentary on the book of Matthew helps explain it:

> The opinion that the term means 'jailors' is unwarranted; it means torturers. They may at the same time be jailors, but they are more than that. Among the tortures anciently applied to imprisoned debtors were: dragging about heavy chains, near-starving, excessive labor, and carnificia or bodily tortures proper.

Augsburg Publishing House, 1943

In other words, those refusing to forgive experience a great deal of suffering, whatever form it takes.

Some have suggested that this passage refers to hell, where both the tormentors and the tormented are kept. But this cannot be true because hell is forever. Thankfully, Jesus gave the unforgiving man a time limit. "And his master was angry, and delivered him to the torturers *until* he should pay all that was due to him" (verse 34, emphasis added).

There is no "until" in hell. Jesus said the torment would continue *until* the unforgiving man forgave, and that it would stop when "he should pay all that was due to him." To Jesus, forgiveness is a debt, something we owe to others because we have received such incredible forgiveness ourselves. He taught this parable to deliver a strong yank upward. While tough, it paints a vivid picture of the misery caused by unforgiveness. Whatever "torturers" means, I am positive I do not want to experience it!

Debtors to a Forgiving God

To help us along, consider the extent to which God went in order to purchase our forgiveness. He visited earth via the miraculous virgin birth, walked among us, personally felt our pain and suffered every conceivable temptation, yet without sinning. Then He allowed the very people He came to redeem to whip and abuse Him, finally hanging Him on a cross—the worst instrument of torture known to the ancient world. Our minds cannot fathom the grave moment when Jesus, who was God wrapped in skin, peered into heaven through blood-stained eyes and cried out, "My God, My God, why have You forsaken Me?" (Matthew 27:46).

At high noon over a solemn Jerusalem, nature bowed in grief as a strange, untimely night covered the earth. H.D.M. Spence writes in *The Pulpit Commentary*,

> The narrative does not oblige us to think of anything more than an indescribable and oppressive darkness, which like a vast black pall hung over earth and sea. The effect on the multitude was quickly perceptible. We hear of no more cries of mocking and derision; only just at the end of the three dark hours is the silence broken by the mysterious and awful cry of the Sinless One.

The cross was God's nuclear bomb in the cosmic battle for our souls, a battle that reached its ultimate climax the moment Jesus bowed His bloodied brow and cried, "It is finished!" (John 19:30). From that moment on, the crimson blood of the virgin-born Son of God destroyed Satan's power over all who place their faith in

The cross was God's nuclear bomb in the cosmic battle for our souls.

Him! That includes the power of death, hell and the grave. If God was willing to allow His Son to suffer this terrible death, He expects us to forgive. We have no choice.

To forgive is the core and essence of Christianity. No forgiveness, no Christianity. The evidence of an apple tree is apples. The proof of an orange tree is oranges. *The evidence of Christianity is forgiveness.* A Christian who will not forgive is the same as someone staring at a rainbow and insisting that red is not in the mix. You cannot miss red in a rainbow, and you cannot miss the red stream of forgiveness in Christianity. As recipients of God's forgiveness, we are debtors who must offer it to others.

Okay, there are about as many ways to be offended as there are stars in the sky. It is time for the rubber to meet the road—time to take a hard look at the consequences of unresolved offenses. Let's put some of the most common causes in the crosshairs of honest scrutiny and learn some things.

Follow-up Questions

1. Have you been experiencing health problems that could be linked to bitterness?
2. If your walk with God is not what it used to be, is it possible that you are doing some "jail time" until you forgive someone?
3. Has Christ been trying to get your attention in order to come to terms with an offense?

I encourage you to allow His Spirit to speak to your heart, that you might face and deal with it!

Part 2

Offenses Come in Many Colors

Awake! Be on the alert! Your enemy the devil, like a roaring lion, prowls round looking for someone to devour.

1 Peter 5:8, NEB

5

Jealousy, Greed and Anger

Offenses have torn through mankind's story and left a tragic legacy. Kingdoms have been shaken, lives destroyed and promising potentials blunted by the snarling dogs of offense. The Bible gives many examples to chew on. Let's look at a few.

Jesus' Hometown: Jealousy-Driven Offense

Jesus returned to His hometown of Nazareth at the height of His ministry. As was His habit, He taught in the synagogue and was prepared to release the same dynamic blessing He had released everywhere else. But He offended the townspeople, who asked, "Is this not the carpenter's son? Is not His mother called Mary? And His brothers James, Joses, Simon and Judas?" (Matthew 13:55).

Jesus was faced with familiarity mixed with jealousy. The townsfolk knew His family, had watched Him play in the streets as a little boy and had seen Him grow up among them. But much had transpired since then. He had been baptized by John, experienced His wilderness victory against Satan and was now moving powerfully in the anointing of the Holy Spirit. He was magnetic, gracious, authoritative, appealing and immensely popular. Now this famous, charismatic man who commanded huge crowds and worked mighty miracles stood in front of them, and jealousy reared its ugly head. This prompted Jesus to exclaim, "A prophet will always be held in honour, except in his hometown, and in his own family" (Matthew 13:57, NEB).

The dog of jealousy crept into Nazareth and tragically robbed them. Their attitude was, "Who does He think He is?" Amazingly, even Jesus' family thought He had gone off the deep end. "When His family heard about this, they went to take charge of him, for they said, 'He is out of his mind'" (Mark 3:21, NIV). They, too, could not receive God's message because of jealousy's insidious bite. Instead of rejoicing over what God was doing through Him, the Bible records, "So they were offended at Him" (Matthew 13:57).

Those last six words spelled the fate of an entire community. *So they were offended at Him.* The people of Nazareth paid a high price for their offense. Scripture sadly records, "Now He did not do many mighty works there because of their unbelief" (verse 58). Tragically, many sick, infirm, possessed and desperate people were not healed because jealousy-driven offense hindered the flow of divine power. It cheated His family, friends and all of Nazareth out of a bona fide visitation from God!

Judas: Greed-Driven Offense

Toward the end of His ministry, Jesus visited Bethany and the house of Simon the leper. During His visit, Mary (the sister of Martha and Lazarus), came to Him with an expensive alabaster box full of costly perfume and began pouring it on His head in a beautiful act of worship. The disciples were offended. "Why this waste? For this fragrant oil might have been sold for much and given to the poor" (Matthew 26:8–9).

Christ promptly defended her, suggesting that she had a better understanding of His impending death and resurrection than they did. "For in pouring this fragrant oil on My body, she did it for My burial" (verse 12). Eleven of the twelve disciples received Jesus' words of correction, and their offense passed. But not Judas. A sinister darkness crept over him as the dog of offense closed in. Something snapped on the inside, but the cause is no mystery. Scripture reveals, "He was a thief, and had the money box; and he used to take what was put in it" (John 12:6).

Covetous and dishonest, Judas could not stand to watch what he considered to be a waste. Jesus delivered eleven of His disciples, but Judas was overcome with greed-driven offense. Filled with anger, he stormed out and soon did the unthinkable.

Perhaps calculating how much money he could have made off of the costly perfume, he negotiated with the chief priests an amount for which to betray Jesus:

Then one of the twelve, called Judas Iscariot, went to the chief priests and said, "What are you willing to give me if I deliver Him to you?" And they counted out to him thirty pieces of silver. So from that time he sought opportunity to betray Him.

Matthew 26:14–16

Greed-fueled offense triggered the trap that snapped on Judas' head, and the repercussions were incalculable.

As a pastor, I have seen the offense of greed cause many to stumble. A wife finds out her husband has been going to church and, gasp, tithing! She stumbles over his giving heart and strikes out in rage. Even a simple message on tithing causes some to stumble because they cannot imagine giving to God. "Why this waste?" they ask. To the human perspective, anything valuable given to God is a waste. In reality, He usually gets our leftovers.

Have you ever noticed how a twenty-dollar bill looks small at the mall but huge in church? It reminds me of the story of the hundred-dollar bill and one-dollar bill having a talk.

"Where have you been spending your life?" asked the one-dollar bill.

"Oh," said the hundred-dollar bill, "I have been to the finest places in the world—Europe, tropical resorts, the most lavish restaurants, the finest clothing stores. The fun just never ends. How about you?"

The dollar answered, "Oh, I have mainly been in church."

Just have a clothing drive for the poor sometime and watch what people drop in the box. Although a few bring nice things, most drop in stuff that they would not wear to bed, much less in public. "Why this waste?" they think. But to those who love Him, even giving much is not enough. They gladly say with King David, "Nor will I offer burnt offerings to the LORD my God with that which costs me nothing" (2 Samuel 24:24).

Like a row of dominos, circumstances of cosmic proportion were set into motion when Judas refused to deal with his heart. Lurking in the shadows, the dog of greed-driven offense seized the moment and lunged. The religious leaders knew that his loyalty could be bought, and he betrayed Jesus for a paltry thirty pieces of silver. The end result was Christ's crucifixion. And later, filled with horror over his actions, Judas took his own life.

> Later, filled with horror over his actions, Judas took his own life.

This story illustrates how offenses can move us to do things we think we would never do, shocking even ourselves. When Judas resisted Jesus' words of correction, the familiar pattern of offense began to unfold. Ultimately, Satan pulled the string, and the box fell on his head.

Absalom: Anger-Driven Offense

A tragic chain of events that began with a sordid, incestuous affair changed King David and the nation of Israel forever. It began simply enough. Amnon, one of David's sons, became convinced that he was in love with his beautiful half-sister Tamar. In reality, he was "in lust." Lust is always easy to spot because it does not understand the word *wait*. "Amnon was so distressed over his sister Tamar that he became sick" (2 Samuel 13:2).

To end his frustration, a friend convinced Amnon to pretend he was ill and then call Tamar to bring him food and drink. Unfortunately, Amnon took his friend's bad advice.

51

When Tamar arrived his lust got the better of him, and he abused her sexually. To make matters worse, he rejected her cruelly afterward, as lust usually does. Scripture records his abysmal response to her: "Then Amnon hated her exceedingly, so that the hatred with which he hated her was greater than the love with which he had loved her. And Amnon said to her, 'Arise, be gone!'" (2 Samuel 13:15).

By Old Testament law he should have married her, and here is where the plot thickens. Tamar also had a brother named Absalom, who knew something was wrong and asked, "Has Amnon your brother been with you? But now hold your peace, my sister. He is your brother; do not take this thing to heart" (verse 20). In other words, "Don't worry about it; I'll handle this in my own special way." Absalom was deeply offended by what had happened and nursed the offense for two full years until it turned into full-blown hatred.

> Absalom was deeply offended by what had happened and nursed the offense for two full years until it turned into full-blown hatred.

"For Absalom hated Amnon, because he had forced his sister Tamar" (verse 22).

One oddity to the story is the strange response, or lack of response, from King David. When word of the atrocity reached him, Scripture records: "But when Kind David heard of all these things, he was very angry" (verse 21). Angry? Yes. Did something? No. King David, father of both Tamar and Amnon, did *absolutely nothing*. No justice was meted out, and this fueled Absalom's offense.

Before long, he began to plot Amnon's murder. One day, Absalom hosted what we might call a sheepshearers' convention. It was supposed to be a time of merriment and fun for those who toiled in the sheep business. All of his brothers were invited to attend, including Amnon. Absalom, however, had told his servants, "Watch now, when Amnon's heart is merry with wine, and when I say to you, 'Strike Amnon!' then kill him" (verse 28). At the opportune moment Absalom gave the command, and Amnon was murdered in cold blood.

Panic ensued. Messengers rushed to David informing him of the tragedy. Now a fugitive, Absalom fled to Geshur.

After three long years Absalom approached Joab, the captain of David's armies, to persuade the king to allow his return to Jerusalem. Joab succeeded. But again, David's behavior was odd. Absalom sat in Jerusalem for two long years without once being summoned by his father. Talk about family dysfunction. This is five years without even speaking once! Troubled people trouble people, and Absalom was no exception.

> Troubled people trouble people, and Absalom was no exception.

Frustrated by his unsuccessful attempts to gain David's audience, he foolishly ordered Joab's field to be set on fire. "So he said to his servants, 'See, Joab's field is near mine, and he has barley there; go and set it on fire.' And Absalom's servants set the field on fire" (2 Samuel 14:30). The offended start fires all the time—fires of gossip, discord, hatred and so on. But you do not mess with the Joabs of the world, as Absalom would one day find out.

In the meantime, Joab decided that losing fields was not worth it. Again, he intervened in the father-son problem, persuading David to see Absalom. But the meeting was stiff at best. "And when he had called for Absalom, he came to the king and bowed himself on his face to the ground before the king. Then the king kissed Absalom" (verse 33). The kiss was all, but it is hard to blame David. After all, the son before him had killed his own brother.

Absalom left unchanged, and the poison of bitterness grew steadily in the dark chambers of his heart. Soon, an idea hatched out of his offended spirit that would spell his doom. Overthrow Dad! That's it! Get revenge! After all, he was known for his looks, dripped with charisma and was the king's son. You probably know the rest of the story. He began standing at the city gates, intercepting those who came to King David with legal cases.

> Moreover Absalom would say, "Oh, that I were made judge in the land, and everyone who has any suit or cause would come to me; then I would give him justice." . . . So Absalom stole the hearts of the men of Israel.
>
> 2 Samuel 15:4, 6

Seemingly overnight Absalom successfully manipulated half the kingdom. Selfish and self-absorbed, he cared only about his own hurt and pain, not the people he used.

A mutiny ensued. Civil war erupted. It is difficult to imagine the mighty King David fleeing his own kingdom pursued by a crazed son and weeping from a broken heart, but he did.

Soon the war turned, and Absalom was forced to flee on the back of a mule—at this point, a mule riding a mule. While passing under a huge terebinth tree, his famous hair became entangled in the branches. The mule kept going, leaving the man ironically hung up by his hair! Then Joab (remember that field Absalom set on fire?) found him helplessly dangling and ended his bitter life with a sword—a grisly finish for the son of a king.

Absalom's legacy? Thousands of innocent people were killed. Israel's testimony for God was tainted before a watching pagan world. A lifetime of loss fell to thousands of survivors who never saw dads, sons or husbands again—all because of one man's offense!

Jealousy, greed and anger-driven offenses are just a few examples of how this craftiest of thieves can appear from anywhere at any time and blindside

Selfish and self-absorbed, he cared only about his own hurt and pain, not the people he used.

the unsuspecting. That is why we must learn to handle offense successfully, including learning to bring your anguish to God. We will look at this in depth in Part 3.

But what if you cannot take your pain and hurt to God because you feel that *He* is the one who has offended you? We will consider this in the next chapter.

Follow-up Questions

1. Has jealousy caused you to be offended? If so, is it affecting an important relationship?
2. Have you been trapped by a greed-driven offense? How can you break its power?
3. Like Absalom, are you angry over unrequited justice?

If so, I encourage you to be honest with yourself and declare a moratorium on it. Allow the Holy Spirit to give you a plan of action, and then resolve to obey. You will not regret it.

6

Failed Expectations

One of the most sinister eroders of faith is offense toward God. This may sound silly to you. *Offended by God?* How could someone be offended by a perfect God? It happens all the time! Thousands have left churches and even Christianity itself because they have taken offense with God.

How does it happen? Offense toward God usually boils down to failed expectations. Failed expectations happen when God does not do *what* we thought He would, *when* we thought He should, the *way* we thought He would. It can cause even the best of us to stumble.

A loved one stands in need of a miracle. A prodigal (wasteful, reckless) child needs to come home. A new business needs to take off and fly. *You just know it is going to happen.* Your faith is high. You are standing on the promises of the Bible. Others are standing in agreement with you, expressing the same level of faith and expectancy that you sense in your own heart. The setting seems perfect for a miracle.

Then, pow! The spouse passes away, the child does not return home, the new business venture fails. Failed expectations slug you in the gut. You are crushed. Your mind reels. *Where was God?* Like a red-hot arrow, the thought shoots through your mind, "How could He have disappointed me this way? Didn't He hear me? I just knew. . . ." Feelings of disappointment and disillusionment wash over you. Cast down and weary, your faith weakens as nagging questions flood your mind with doubt.

> Offense toward God usually boils down to failed expectations.

In short, your faith in God has been scandalized. Subtle erosion begins to eat away at your trust in the Lord. Failed expectations, like mild earthquake tremors, begin to shake imperceptibly the promises of God from under your feet. Prayer becomes difficult. You think, *If God did not answer this prayer, how can I know He will answer anything, or that He is even listening to me at all?* The problem is that you are offended by the God you were *expecting.*

> The problem is that we are offended by the God we were expecting.

Scripture is filled with examples of men and women whose faith was dealt staggering blows. Some sailed through it; others sank into despair. Let's take a look at one of them.

The Great Leader with a Dirty Secret

Naaman, commander of the king's armies in Syria, was a powerful, influential man. He oversaw a huge and successful military force. If alive today, Naaman would be at the top of every Who's Who list. A man's man, he seemed to have it all. But Naaman harbored a dark secret. There was one thing in his illustrious life that he could not control, handle or fix. He was a leper.

God often chooses unlikely ways to reach us. In one of Naaman's military expeditions a young Israeli girl was taken captive. She ultimately became a servant to Naaman's wife, and his family secret soon was exposed. Having learned of his leprosy, the young girl told him about a prophet in Israel who could heal him. *Could it be true?* Naaman went to the king of Syria and gained permission to visit the famous prophet Elisha.

Remember, *failed expectations* are the primary cause of most offenses toward God. Either our expectations come from a true understanding of God and His ways, or they are birthed in the seedbed of presumption. They spring either from a legitimate promise of God or from wishful thinking. Naaman's story is a classic example of the latter.

His problem was not with God. It was wrapped up in that little four-word phrase, "I said to myself."

The mighty commander arrived at Elisha's house in impressive pomp and splendor. Horsemen, chariots and servants surrounded him in a great show of power. I can just picture him knocking on Elisha's door with this impressive entourage behind him. Scripture reveals that he was filled with presumptuous expectations of exactly how Elisha would bring about his healing. Yet to his shock, the crusty old prophet did not do anything that Naaman expected. It began with Elisha not bothering to come to the door! "And Elisha sent a messenger to him" (2 Kings 5:10).

Expectation number one popped like a big balloon. Naaman presumed that the prophet would greet and receive him personally like the great man that he was. But his problem was rooted in a little conversation he had had with himself on the way to the prophet's house. Listen closely to the words: "'Indeed,' I said to myself, 'He will surely come out to me'" (verse 11). His problem was not with God. It was wrapped up in that little four-word phrase, "I said to myself."

> When we "say to ourselves" apart from God's leading, we are set up for scandalized faith.

Strike one. The first failed expectation hit him like a Muhammad Ali punch in the gut. His face growing red with rage, he already was beginning to struggle with the contradiction between presumption and hard, cold reality. Naaman had said some things "to himself" on the way to the prophet's house that set him up to be offended with God. We all have expectations, and we should. When it comes to prayer, however, Scripture teaches us to leave *how* God is going to answer up to Him. When we "say to ourselves" apart from God's leading, we are set up for scandalized faith.

You Cannot Put God in a Box

God is very creative. Just follow Jesus through the gospels and you will find an innovative God at work. He healed a blind man by spitting in the dirt and putting the mud on his eyes. He healed two more blind men by touching their eyes with His fingers. A deaf man was healed by placing His fingers in his ears, and then spitting and touching his tongue (see Matthew 9:27–30; Mark 7:32–35; John 9:1–7).

Virtually every miracle of Jesus was uniquely executed. My point? *You cannot place God in a box.* As soon as you think you have Him figured out, He does it another way. Naaman was about to learn this the hard way.

He also assumed *the method* Elisha would use to heal him. When you read what he expected, you cannot blame the guy for having a great imagination! Scripture says that Naaman expected Elisha to "stand and call on the name of the LORD his God, and wave his hand over the place, and heal the leprosy" (2 Kings 5:11).

Expectation number two evaporated into the thin air of disillusionment. Elisha did not dramatically call on God or wave his hand like a magician over the leprosy. Instead, he told Naaman to go for a swim. "Go and wash in the Jordan seven times, and your flesh shall be restored to you, and you shall be clean" (verse 10).

I can almost hear the inner rumblings of this stunned military genius. "How dare he! Doesn't he know who I am?" Adding insult to injury, Elisha sent him to the muddy Jordan River, which Naaman vehemently protested. If he was going to have to dip down seven times, why not at least do so in a classy river! "'Are not the Abanah and the Pharpar, the rivers of Damascus, better than all the waters of Israel? Could I not wash in them and be clean?' So he turned and went away in a rage" (verse 12).

Two Birds with One Stone

This is a classic case of failed expectations. God did not do *what* Naaman thought he would in the *way* he thought he should, and Naaman became offended. But God knows what He is doing, and it is often more than meets the eye. His inscrutable wisdom exposed another leprosy in Naaman's life: *pride*. Naaman's pride was wounded, and like a divine X-ray machine God's method brought it to light.

But why fool with that? Naaman simply needed physical healing, right?

God wanted to reach Naaman's soul as well, which was far more important, and to do that required humbling him. Pride is the first sin recorded in the Bible. It is the sin that brought Satan's downfall. It is the horse that pulls the carriage of catastrophe, a false pick-me-up that later drops us. Pride almost kept Naaman from both a life-changing miracle and a personal encounter with God!

Like Naaman, we, too, are infected with pride. We can become offended when God asks us to admit that we were wrong and ask forgiveness or to forgive someone who has hurt us. We would much rather have a magic wand waved over the hurt caused by offense—a quick fix; the easy way out. But there is no magic wand for an offense; rather, there is healing only through obedience.

> There is no magic wand for an offense; there is healing only through obedience.

At the encouragement of his servants, Naaman gave in and did what the prophet said. Down to the muddy Jordan they went. Feeling foolish, Naaman slowly trod into the cold, rushing water. Each time he dipped in the river, a little more pride was washed away. Once. Twice. Three times—each time glancing to see who watched. Four. Five. Six.

I have nothing in Scripture to support what I believe happened after dip number six, so allow me a bit of poetic license. He no longer looked to see who watched. By now it did not matter, because something deep within him began to change. *The high walls of pride began to crumble under the battering ram of obedience.* He trembled. This was it, the big one, the moment of truth. *I am healed,* he must have thought, *or I die a horrible death; I have been a fool for coming here, or it was God.* It grew very quiet. None of the huge entourage of onlookers moved. Breathing deep, down he went. Pushing out for the last time, he immediately looked at where the leprosy had been. Gone. Baby's skin. Pink and clean. He rubbed his eyes and looked again. Completely healed! "And his flesh was restored like the flesh of a little child, and he was clean" (verse 14).

Faith in the true and living God washed over him with greater force than the cold waters of the muddy Jordan. From that moment on, this mighty man of valor was healed physically and joined to God by faith. Two birds with one miracle!

Perhaps you have lost a loved one to death, lost a job, a spouse has walked out on you or some other gut-wrenching, mind-numbing, faith-crushing event has befallen you, and you are wondering where God is. *He is there.* I know you may not feel His presence, and you may feel angry and confused. Far be it from me to be preachy or to imagine I can fully comprehend your pain. But allow me to drop a few thoughts your way that I think will help.

A Dirty Windshield on a Rainy Night

In your offense toward God there are things you cannot see right now because you are limited as a human being. How often I have wished I could understand events that I simply could not comprehend without the passing of time! And I know some mysteries will remain so until I reach the other side. Even Paul confessed to seeing through a glass darkly—the equivalent of trying to see through a dirty windshield on a rainy night. You strain to see through the windshield of your pain, but the pelting rain of disappointment and howling winds of discouragement blind you. So often, especially in pain, we can barely see the road at all. But I can tell you four things for certain.

- He loves you.
- He sees your pain.
- He cares.
- Time is a great revealer.

Give it time. Though you cannot see it, your momentary affliction "is working . . . a far more exceeding and eternal weight of glory" (2 Corinthians 4:17).

Offense with God can be tough to overcome, but what about when the one who causes the offense is you? You mess up, you fail, you let yourself and the Lord down and stumble over your own actions. What then? It happened to one of Jesus' favorite disciples. In the next chapter we will take a look at one of my favorite Bible people and how he overcame personal failure.

Follow-up Questions

1. Do you feel God has somehow failed you? If so, how?

2. Have you "said to yourself" some things that have set you up for failed expectations? What are they?

3. Is God directing you to do a "humbling" thing in order to be healed? What is the worst that could happen if you do it? Is your fear valid?

I encourage you to let go of specific expectations and allow God to move in His own time and way!

7

Peter—The Bitter Sting
of Personal Failure

Of Jesus' disciples, Simon Peter was certainly the "character." Impetuous, reckless and salty, Peter usually managed to be the center of attention and the life of the party—and the disciple who stuck his foot in his mouth with great regularity. On the Mount of Transfiguration, for example, Peter suggested to Jesus that the disciples build three tabernacles—one each for Jesus, Moses and Elijah. Imagine—Elijah and Moses appear walking with Jesus, and Peter suggests building dwellings for them! Mark 9:6 tells us that he said this when "he did not know what to say." I chuckle at the honesty of Scripture. When Peter did not know what to say, *he said.* Overconfident, he misjudged his own strength on more than one occasion.

Peter was also the most impulsive disciple. It was he who stepped out on the water and walked toward Jesus (see Matthew 14:26–29), who cut off the servant's ear at the arrest of Jesus (see Mark 14:47) and who blurted out that Jesus was the Christ, the Son of the living God, only to be rebuked by the Lord moments later for trying to deter Him from the cross (see Mark 8:27–33).

And, of course, following Jesus' prediction that all the disciples would be offended and forsake Him, it was Peter who said, "Even if all are made to stumble, yet I will not be" (Mark 14:29). Jesus knowingly replied, "Assuredly, I say to you that today, even this night, before the rooster crows twice, you will deny Me three times" (verse 30). In classic fashion, Peter stuck his foot in his mouth again. "If I have to die with You, I will not deny You!" (verse 31).

Soon thereafter, following Jesus' gut-wrenching Gethsemane experience, a large crowd armed with swords and clubs approached the small band of disciples. Judas, a former disciple and the leader of the mob, approached Jesus and kissed Him, identifying Jesus as the one to apprehend. The Greek word that describes Judas' kiss goes beyond a casual greeting.

> Like an early morning fog, courage evaporated and faith withdrew in fear to the dark shadows of their souls.

It was the affectionate, fervent greeting of an intimate friend, making the betrayal particularly cruel.

Instantly caught up in the emotion of the moment, Peter drew his sword at the high priest's servant and sliced off his ear. Though rebuked by Jesus for his action, he had not fled yet. But when the mob seized Jesus, "all the disciples forsook Him and fled" (Matthew

26:56). Like an early morning fog, courage evaporated and faith withdrew in fear to the dark shadows of their souls.

Yet Peter remained at a distance watching the terrible events unfold. At this point in the narrative the Bible zooms in for a close-up on him, because Peter's was the strongest promise; and his would be the strongest denial.

Three Betrayals and a Glance

Peter drew his sword before an angry mob, but only hours later he shrank in fear before a servant girl. While standing in the courtyard of the high priest's home where Jesus had been taken, a young damsel observed, "You also were with Jesus of Nazareth" (Mark 14:67). Knowing others were listening, he said, "I neither know nor understand what you are saying" (verse 68).

Peter could not believe his own words, yet more would come. As he walked toward the gateway, the girl cried out, "This is one of them." Fear-driven denial again poured from his lips, and again he denied it: 'I do not know the Man!'" But Peter did not stop there. The third time he was accused of being Jesus' disciple, he completely lost control. "He began to curse and swear, saying, 'I do not know this Man of whom you speak!'" (Matthew 26:69–71).

One of Jesus' inner three, His top man, the one who first declared Him the Christ, bit the dust and bit it hard, scandalizing his own faith. He tripped and fell over his own error, spiraling deep down into shame and condemnation of his own making. As Peter spat out his third denial, Jesus was escorted past him. Scripture records that He turned and looked at Peter. I can just imagine the howling dogs of conviction ripping into Peter's stung conscience. No wonder he "went out and wept bitterly" (verse 72).

Does his experience have a familiar ring to it? You thought you could handle something; you were sure you could stand. Then, *wham!* Your faith collapsed in the heat of a trial or temptation. You were broadsided when you said or did the unthinkable. Now disappointment with yourself dogs you unmercifully.

> Personal failure covers us in clouds of shame that can drive us away from church, friends and even God.

Personal failure covers us in clouds of shame that can drive us away from church, friends and even God. Sinking in the quicksand of defeat, we wonder how our faith failed or if our experience with God was real at all! *If it was,* we ask, *how could this have happened?* Personal failure can take a person for the ride of his life on the roller coaster of condemnation.

Jesus knew Peter's fall was coming and forewarned him. "Simon, Simon! Indeed, Satan has asked for you, that he may sift you as wheat" (Luke 22:31).

Sift means "to shake." When a farmer sifted wheat in biblical times, he tossed it high in the air. The wind blew off the chaff, allowing the pure grain to fall to the ground. Jesus was telling Peter that Satan was going to violently toss his faith in the air in order to scandalize and destroy it. This is why He assured Peter that He had prayed for his faith to survive the onslaught (see verse 32). But it would take several appearances from the risen Christ before Peter got over it!

Easter Changes Things!

A few days after Peter's fall, in the pre-dawn hours of the first Easter morning, a small band of women walked mournfully to the borrowed tomb to anoint Jesus' body for burial. They found that the stone had already been rolled away—not to let Him out, as they thought, but to let them in. Since He later walked through doors and walls and was no longer subject to natural law, it is safe to assume that He did not need for the stone to be moved. An angel sitting inside told the startled women that Jesus had risen from the dead. He continued, "Go quickly and tell His disciples . . . He is going before you into Galilee; there you will see Him" (Matthew 28:7).

Sometimes you have to watch Scripture closely. Small statements that actually pack huge punches can shoot right past you. This was never truer than with two particular words found at the end of Mark's account of the angel's declaration to the astonished women that Matthew did not include: "Go, tell His disciples—*and Peter*—that He is going before you into Galilee; there you will see Him" (Mark 16:7, emphasis added).

Jesus was raised from the dead. Satan, death, hell and the grave were defeated, our redemption was forever purchased, and the world was under a brand-new grace. But heaven's attention was focused on the restoration of one solitary, downcast disciple! Jesus watched Peter fall flat on his face, yet Fed-Exed a special angelic telegram of encouragement: *Go tell Peter I still love him. I have not rejected him. His failure was not final. Because I live he can face tomorrow, even after a terrible defeat!*

There Is Nothing Back There

After His resurrection, Jesus made several miraculous appearances to the disciples. In spite of irrefutable proof of His resurrection and the angel's encouraging words, Peter still seemed unable to shake the lingering bite of sin. Like guilty children, he and some of the other disciples fled to what they knew best before meeting Jesus—the sea and fishing. "Simon Peter said to them, 'I am going fishing.' They said to him, 'We are going with you also'" (John 21:3). Like many who struggle with personal failure, they tried to return to their old lives. Fishing was all they had known before they met Jesus, yet they soon discovered a familiar truth.

> There is nothing back there. You cannot go back because you are not the same.

There is nothing back there. You cannot go back because you are not the same. You discover God has closed the sea behind you! Scripture records, "That night they caught nothing" (verse 3).

Like the disciples, we, too, seek to hide in the shadows of our old lives after failing God. Our Bibles become dust collectors while we leave church, Christian friends and fellowship with God behind. But it does not work. You cannot put your finger on it, but the surroundings seem eerily different. People connections you once had no longer jive. You find yourself in a sort of Twilight Zone, hanging between two worlds with the inability to connect with either. *You catch nothing.*

"Cast" Sheep

One of the things that I love about Jesus is that He is forever watching over His sheep. In His parable of the Good Shepherd, one out of one hundred sheep turned up missing. Jesus said that the shepherd immediately left the ninety-nine to find the one (see Matthew 18:11–13).

There was a reason for his urgency that all real shepherds understand. Sheep are not smart animals, which is why they need a shepherd in the first place. When a sheep wanders from the flock he will eventually lie down, which is no problem for most animals. But when a sheep rolls onto his back he cannot roll back over. In a matter of a few hours, gases begin to build up in his body, causing him to bloat. Frantically flailing, they are helpless to regain their equilibrium. Blood flow to their limbs is cut off. This condition is called "cast." A cast sheep will die if the shepherd does not find him quickly.

> A cast sheep will die if the shepherd does not find him quickly.

God's people are the same, which is why Jesus comes to us so quickly in our failure and despair. Peter was no exception. He was "cast." Stricken by his failure, he was sinking in spite of seeing the risen Christ several times. He no doubt believed his calling was ruined. This is why Scripture records that Jesus came to the Sea of Galilee and once again found His "cast" disciples. He stood on the shore and called to them, "Children, have you any food?" (John 21:5).

Sound familiar? He also stands on the shore of your frustration, anger and bewilderment and gently asks, "Have you found anything here?" The answer is only too obvious. Just like the disciples who were staring at empty nets through bloodshot eyes, Jesus' question probes deep down and asks the obvious: "Have you found meaning in your past? Does it do for you what it used to? Is anything out there?" All they could choke out was, "No."

Peter's Moment of Truth

Still unrecognized by them, the lone figure on the shore next instructed Peter and his weary comrades to cast their net on the right side of the boat. Scratching their heads, they obeyed. They had caught nothing all night, but something about the command rang strangely familiar. Suddenly, as if pulled by a magnet, thousands of fish flooded their nets to the breaking point. John quickly connected the dots. He remembered another fruitless night about three years before and a similar command from . . . *Jesus!* "It is the Lord!" he cried (John 21:7).

Peter plunged into the water first. Sick and tired of the whip of condemnation lashing his conscience, *he had to get things right.* It often takes several visitations from the Lord to heal a bitten conscience, but this time a beautiful restoration waited.

When Jesus Meddles, It Is for Our Own Good

With the sound of fish crackling over a small fire, Jesus looked His fallen disciple straight in the eye and asked, "'Simon, son of Jonah, do you love Me more than these?'" (John 21:15). In this verse the word Jesus used for love was *agape,* which is God's kind of love. It is not based on feelings, natural affinity or inclinations. Agape love is given "in spite of" not "because of." It is unconditional, embraces the unlovely, is a choice on the

72

lover's part and does not depend on response or lack of it. "While we were yet sinners, Christ died for us" (Romans 5:8, NASB).

In using this word, Jesus was forcing an issue with Peter, who had once bragged that though the others would leave Jesus, he would not. Jesus added the stinger: "Do you love Me more than these?" I can just picture Peter staring at the ground, fidgeting, knowing his boast of perfect love had failed miserably. Humbled, Peter came face-to-face with himself.

> Humbled, Peter came face-to-face with himself.

"Yes, Lord; You know that I love You" (verse 15). Unlike Jesus, Peter used the word *phileo* in his response. *Phileo* means "to have a tender affection for, be fond of, or to care for." It is not absolute, like *agape*. Peter knew this was closer to the truth. Jesus then repeated the question a second time and got the same *phileo* response from Peter. Both times, Jesus commanded him: "Feed My sheep" (verses 15 and 16).

Finally, Jesus asked Peter the question a third time, but this time changed it. "Simon, son of Jonah, do you love [*phileo*] Me?" (verse 17). Another zinger straight to Peter's heart. Jesus wanted to know if Peter even had *phileo* affection for him. This is why the Bible says, "Peter was grieved because He said to him the third time, 'Do you love [*phileo*] Me?'" (verse 17).

Jesus was not playing cruel mind games with His discouraged disciple. Rather, Jesus was teaching that when we are truthful with ourselves, we also can forgive ourselves.

I believe Jesus was bringing Peter to just that—the place of forgiving himself. He was pushing the point so that Peter could accept where he truly was—faults, failures and all. Exasperated, Peter blurted out, "Lord, You know all things; You know that I love [*phileo*] You." And Jesus said to him, "Feed My sheep" (verse 17).

> **When we are truthful with ourselves, we also can forgive ourselves.**

Such refreshing honesty from Peter! In one fell swoop, Jesus gave His fallen disciple the opportunity to reaffirm his commitment, forgive himself and continue in his calling. Three denials from Peter, three questions from Jesus and three honest answers brought restoration.

You Must Forgive Yourself

Sometimes the hardest person to let off the hook is yourself. I remember a personal failure where I felt I had really let down the Lord. I went to God in prayer, repented and felt His forgiveness. Yet, like Peter, I could not seem to get fully past it. One day God gently impressed my heart with a question: *Are you greater than My blood?* My response was immediate. "Of course not!" But He replied, *Then why do you refuse to forgive yourself for what My shed blood has washed away?* That settled it. Sometimes the greatest hindrance to forgiveness is in your refusal to forgive *you*. After personal failure the time must come when you look in the mirror and forgive yourself!

Peter's failure was not final. His finest hour waited just around the corner— and so does yours! Because he was able to forgive himself, he emerged from his valley of defeat stronger than ever, strengthened his brethren and became one of the most powerful voices in the history of the world. It was Peter who soon stood and preached the thundering message of repentance to thousands of people following the mighty outpouring of the Holy Spirit on the day of Pentecost. The grace of God so strongly rested on him that his very shadow healed the sick on the streets of Jerusalem (see Acts 2, 5)! And his two let-

> After personal failure, the time must come when you look in the mirror and forgive yourself!

ters to the churches (1 and 2 Peter) stagger the intellects of scholars to this day. In the same way He restored Peter, Jesus can restore you from the crippling offense of personal failure!

But there is yet another kind of offense that many do not consider. In fact, it is one of the most sinister because it is one of the subtlest. We will take a look at this type of offense in the following chapter.

Follow-up Questions

1. Have you experienced a personal failure that you find difficult to get past?
2. Do you believe deep down that God has forgiven you? If not, why not? If so, have you forgiven yourself? What is stopping you?
3. Have you sought to return to your old life because of your failure? If so, what do you suspect Christ is saying to you?

I encourage you to refuse to allow failure to define you. Remember Moses the murderer? How about Abraham's lies? And what about David's adultery? These are just a few of the personal failures the Bible records. Yet all of these men arose from the ashes of failure and changed the world. So can you!

8

Secondhand Offenses

Research in recent years has revealed the dangers of secondhand smoke. Doctors now say it is more detrimental for non-smokers to inhale secondhand smoke than it is for smokers to inhale the original tar and nicotine. A non-smoker who lives with a smoker can sustain more long-term lung damage. Likewise, when an offended person shares his offense with someone who is not a party to it, the listener can catch a "secondhand offense" and become infected with the same disease—only worse.

Think of it like this. When a virus mutates, scientists must go back to the drawing board and find a cure for the new strain. The original cure will not touch the mutation. This happens every year with each new strain of flu that cannot be treated by the current vaccine. It is a brand-new enemy. Only time and careful attention can bring the new cure to light. In short, the mutation is often worse than the original.

Likewise, another part of the hapless trail left by unresolved offenses is *contagion*. Offended people carry the equivalent of a spiritual flu, and it often gains strength the more it is spread. This "flu-like" offense is transferred primarily through words. Do you remember James' description of the tongue? "And the tongue is a fire, a world of iniquity. The tongue is so set among our members that it defiles the whole body, and sets on fire the course of nature; and it is set on fire by hell" (James 3:6).

James goes on to describe the way Christians can "bless our God and Father" in one breath, then turn and "curse men" with the next (James 3:9–10). The word *curse* comes from a word that means "to doom or to wish evil against a person." So a Christian can praise God one moment, and the next he or she can wish or speak evil against another human being! Cursing someone through backbiting, gossip, slander or criticism is one way the dogs of offense are unchained to lash out and spread a lethal infection.

> Cursing someone through backbiting, gossip, slander or criticism is one way the dogs of offense are unchained to lash out and spread a lethal infection.

Sometimes I wish God had given us "earlids." They would make it so much easier to screen out gossip, slander, backbiting and the like. Since, however, He did not create such a thing, we must be responsible for screening what we hear. Keeping this in mind, we must remember several things before listening to an offended person. Let's call them *The Three Don'ts of a Listener.*

Don't Listen to a One-Sided Story

The dogs of offense lunge from the shadows through the one-sided story of an offended person. Why? Because while the report of an offended person can be very convincing, it is always skewed by his or her pain, and that assures you are not getting the full story. Angry words are spewed out of a bitter heart that has not yet responded to the grace of God. This colors the story, shading and embellishing the facts. It is like putting on a pair of red sunglasses. The world is seen in shades of red, instead of through the true, complete palette of colors. A bitter tale is a one-sided, offense-driven story tainted by hurt and anger.

> A bitter tale is a one-sided, offense-driven story tainted by hurt and anger.

With unresolved offenses, the truth usually lies somewhere in between. You can take it to the bank: There is another side to every story. It is important, therefore, to be careful about what you listen to and how much stock you put into it before hearing the other side of the story.

Why does this matter? Because the offender can become unfairly colored in the eyes of the secondhand listener before both sides are heard. This is not to say that we cannot hear stories of offense and still remain neutral, but more times than not the contagion spreads. Counselors who deal regularly with offense issues know that every story has two sides. Yet the unwary often pick up an offense after hearing just one side. King Solomon warned, "He who answers a matter before he hears it [both sides], it is folly and shame to him" (Proverbs 18:13). When both sides are not heard, the alleged offender is hastily tried and found guilty in the court of public opinion.

We listeners bear a responsibility to be fair. Solomon again warns of the consequences of listening to just one side. "The words of a talebearer [gossip] are like tasty trifles [wounds], and they go down into the inmost body [rooms of the belly]" (Proverbs 26:22).

> When both sides are not heard, the alleged offender is hastily tried and found guilty in the court of public opinion.

Gossip can be powerful! The one-sided story of an offended person *wounds* the listener. Words of offense go down into your soul just as food goes down into your stomach. They are ingested (taken in) and then digested (broken down). Once you let them in, bitter words become part of you. Like hooks in the heart, the skewed report of an offended gossip is difficult to forget.

I was once in a room with several well-known preachers who had gathered for a conference—I was a little shot among big shots. During the conversation, an off-the-cuff comment was made about someone I had regularly watched on television who had often been a great encouragement to me. I remember being surprised at what was said because it was very critical. The meeting moved on and nothing more was said—but what I had heard stuck in my memory like a catchy bumper sticker.

> The meeting moved on and nothing more was said—but what I had heard stuck in my memory like a catchy bumper sticker.

Months went by and I did not think much more about it. Then

one Sunday morning while getting ready for church something struck me: For weeks, I had not watched the criticized preacher. The Holy Spirit seemed to prod me, *Why aren't you watching Brother _____ anymore?* It quickly dawned on me. The evil report had made an impact. A period had been replaced with a question mark in my mind. The critical comment had gone down into my "inmost body" and shaded my opinion of the one from whom I had once received blessings. Words are so powerful!

Then and there, I repented of my unfair judgment and experienced immediate peace. I also was able to receive from his ministry again. I later learned that the person who had criticized this minister had issues with him and had not handled them biblically. He was bitter and it came out—right in the middle of a Christian conference and among people who loved and served God. Like a victim of secondhand smoke, I became a victim of secondhand offense. It happens all the time, which leads to the second *don't* of a listener.

Don't Pick It Up!

Another aspect of contagion is the risk of "picking up the offense" from the offended party. This goes beyond just having your opinion of the person colored. When you pick up an offense you become offended, angry and even vengeful, just like the one who told you about it!

Their offense becomes *your* offense. Like catching the flu, you literally catch their offense. Even though the situation had nothing to do with you, you become angry, judgmental and critical of the offender as if it had!

In real life, we would never let someone with a flu virus blow or sneeze directly in our faces. Yet we allow embittered people to spew their offenses into our hearts and minds without wincing. We take their sides without knowing if what we are hearing is totally accurate. A person's story can sound true, look true and seem true, yet be partially true or even completely false. In fact, many conflicts come from our being infected with an offense from a one-sided story that we had no business hearing in the first place.

> Many conflicts come from our being infected with an offense from a one-sided story that we had no business hearing in the first place.

When the offended gives an evil report—usually to someone close to him—the secondhand listener runs the risk of picking up the offense. He becomes infected with secondhand anger, along with the other goodies that accompany an offense. I have seen the secondhand offended become more infected than the one who told him or her about it! It is like that mutated flu virus that turns into an even stronger strain.

It is not fair, right or scriptural to judge someone without getting both sides of the story. You would not want to be treated that way, and neither would I—which leads to the third *don't* of a listener.

Don't Be an Enabler

When you take up someone else's offense, you are not doing the person any favors. You may think you are, but you are not. You are not proving love or friendship to the offended person, nor are you confirming your loyalty or devotion. You are only enabling your friend or associate to continue in a wrong behavior. Enabling someone who harbors an offense is like enabling someone to continue in a destructive habit.

Think about it a moment. If you reinforce destructive behavior, is that showing true love? You are helping to reinforce the walls around a well-constructed castle of offense. "A brother offended is harder to win than a strong city, and contentions are like the bars of a castle" (Proverbs 18:19). When you become infected with someone else's offense and take sides, you are enabling that person to spread his or her offense through you. Do you want that?

> When you become infected with someone else's offense and take sides, you are enabling that person to spread his or her offense through you. Do you want that?

Infections from secondhand offense are part of the unfortunate damage left by the dog bite of bitter words. You become a carrier. By obeying the other person's pain, the offended are disobeying God—and enabling the person! True love says to an offended friend, "I love you, I really do, but the way I can help you most is to encourage you to go to the one who offended you and work it out. I'll pray for you as you go." We will cover much more of this "Jesus Approach" in Part 3.

Remember the Birds and the Bread Trail?

Let's quickly recap our bread trail to the box illustration from chapter 2. The four pieces of bread leading up to and under a box represent the four stages in the progression of an offense. The box represents the trap of bitterness. Satan, hoping we follow the bread trail, holds a string tied to a stick that props up the box. If we follow the bread trail all the way under, he pulls the string and the box of bitterness falls on our heads.

The first piece of bread leading to the box trap is the initial offense, which brings *indignation*. Someone deeply hurts you, and you are faced with the choice of whether or not to forgive. The second piece of bread is *justification*. This happens when you justify the decision to harbor a grudge by refusing to forgive. Once the decision to justify unforgiveness is made, you move to the third piece of bread, which is the continual rehearsal of the offense, or *visualization*. In the same way a VCR replay button allows the replay of a scene, you repeatedly hit the memory replay button, visualizing the offense over and over again, which only feeds the process. At this point in the cycle, all that remains is to hop under the box for the fourth piece of bread, which is *actualization*. The offense has now become so real that it consumes you. Bitterness takes root in your heart, the enemy pulls the string, and the box falls on your head. You are trapped by the offense.

Once trapped, the fruit of bitterness springs up, defiling many. It manifests in a variety of ways, such as health issues, severed fellowship with God, character assassination of those who offended you and broken relationships in the home, workplace and church. When the real issues are not handled, contagion through secondhand offense is only a matter of time. The testimony of individuals and churches is compromised as a skeptical world watches.

There is a far better solution than these wrong responses. But before we move to positive solutions, let's look at another side to offense that is truly, well . . . *haunting*. In fact, it may be "haunting" you at this very moment.

Follow-up Questions

1. Have you been affected by secondhand offense? If so, how?
2. Have you been spreading secondhand offense? What is Christ telling you to do about it?
3. In what ways have you personally observed the destruction caused by secondhand offense?

I encourage you to resolve that you will do your part to stop secondhand offense in its tracks through becoming a peacemaker.

_9_

Ghosts

I t has been said that what you *achieve* by reaching your destination is not nearly as important as what you *become* getting there. This is so true. If we leave a relationship with unresolved offenses, what we *become* on the way to the next one is crucial to its success or failure. Whether it is a new church, friendship, marriage or business partnership, it is best to arrive whole. The worst thing is to arrive with excess baggage. Not only does baggage weigh you down, but it weighs down everyone else around you as well. This is why it is so important to forgive offenses.

You are the one commodity you take with you everywhere you go. No matter where you go, when you arrive, *you* are there. When I travel, I pack a bag. Upon arrival, everything I have packed arrives with me. As people, we are all "packed bags." All of life's experiences, our

> You are the one commodity you take with you everywhere you go.

responses to each one, how we have processed them and what we have become as a result—all arrive with us as we enter each new situation and meet each new person. This concept could not be illustrated better than through the tragic tale of a man named Herod.

A Really Bad Birthday Party

In the days of Jesus, Herod the Tetrarch ruled Galilee with great cunning—so much so that Jesus referred to him as "that fox" (Luke 13:32). Though crafty, Herod would learn the hard way about the reality of "ghosts." One day, he foolishly fell into a trap that haunted him for the rest of his life. It all began with a rebuke from a salty prophet:

> For Herod had arrested John and chained him in prison at the demand of his wife Herodias, his brother Philip's ex-wife, because John had told him it was wrong for him to marry her.
>
> Matthew 14:3–4, TLB

John the Baptist, Jesus' cousin, never worried about personal popularity or accolades. One day he pointed his long prophetic finger at Herod and his new wife, Herodias, and declared their union adulterous. Their story reads like a modern-day soap opera. Herodias happened to be Herod the Tetrarch's former sister-in-law—his brother Philip's wife. Apparently, an affair with Herod had been instrumental in the destruction of Herodias' marriage to Philip. Hence, John's rebuke.

Herod knew deep inside that John was right, but he was too proud to admit it and receive the words of a prophet. Angry at what John had said, Herod hurled him into prison.

Incidentally, we also imprison people who offend us. We imprison them in the jails of criticism, faultfinding, denunciation, ostracism, hatred and turning others against them.

As John sat in prison, Herod and Herodias followed the familiar bread trail under the box. Indignation, justification, visualization and actualization led to hardcore bitterness, just in time for a birthday party and a fateful dance. The Bible describes the subtle snare laid for Herod:

> We also imprison people who offend us. We imprison them in the jail of criticism, faultfinding, denunciation, ostracism, hatred and turning others against them.

> But at a birthday party for Herod, Herodias' daughter performed a dance that greatly pleased him, so he vowed to give her anything she wanted. Consequently, at her mother's urging, the girl asked for John the Baptist's head on a tray.
>
> Matthew 14:6–8, TLB

In a moment of unguarded lust, Herod made a stupid promise and became caught in a trap from which there was no escape. Entranced by the sensual dance of his stepdaughter, he foolishly promised her anything she desired. The vicious dog of offense suddenly lunged from the dark shadows of his new wife's heart! It seems even this crusty old politician was shocked at her barbaric request for John the Baptist's head on a platter.

The king was grieved, but because of his oath, and because he did not want to back down in front of his guests, he issued the necessary orders. So John was beheaded in the prison, and his head was brought on a tray and given to the girl, who took it to her mother.

Matthew 14:9–10, TLB

This macabre scene branded itself forever on King Herod's guilt-stricken mind. He knew that John did not deserve to die such a horrible death, but alas, a promise was a promise.

This account teaches us a couple of lessons. One: Lust weakens you, causing you to make stupid promises and dumb decisions that you would never consider otherwise. Two: Beauty is a powerful tool that can be used for great good or great evil. Both are worth remembering.

Blinded by Ghosts

After the martyrdom of John, speculation about who Jesus might be was galloping through the kingdom, while His fame and popularity grew at warp speed. Unbeknownst to Herod, his crime against his conscience was about to return to haunt him. The Bible tells us, "At that time Herod the tetrarch heard the reports about Jesus" (Matthew 14:1, NIV).

In a flash, Herod's ghosts jumped to the forefront. "And he said to his attendants, 'This is John the Baptist; he has risen from the dead! That is why miraculous powers are at work in him'" (Matthew 14:2, NIV). Tragically, his unresolved offense with John warped his perception of reality, and he tripped over his own excess baggage. There stood the Christ in all His miracle-working glory, yet Herod could only see a ghost! He could not see who Jesus really was. Rather, he saw only a haunting reflection from his guilty, offense-laden past. Herod could not see Jesus, only John. How sad, because He missed the Savior of the world! A golden opportunity for the salvation of his soul passed by him because the dog of offense still held him by the throat.

Catch that, because a great truth lies in this! You cannot fully receive the new relationships God brings into your life if you are weighed down with baggage from former offenses. The ghosts of relationships past will stand between you and new possibilities. Issues that were never settled blind you to brand-new, God-sent blessings. John the Baptist was dead, but not to Herod. What a tragedy! The greatest human being ever to grace the planet stood before him, but the ghost of John blinded him. Herod was groping in the darkness of the box of bitterness and could not see a thing.

> He could not see who Jesus really was. Rather, he saw only a haunting reflection from his guilty, offense-laden past.

"John" shows up all the time to those who have not forgiven. He haunts them through the gateway of unresolved offenses.

It is easy to know if "John" is around. If he has recently paid you a visit, the following statements are no doubt familiar to you: "You're just like . . . !" Or, "You remind me of . . . !" Or, "Why do I always end up with people like you!" Ring a bell? If "John" has surfaced in your life, either you have said such things, or they have been said to you. Carry-over offenses are weighing you down and causing you to see "John" everywhere you go.

And I guarantee you this: "John" will stay in your new church, new friendships, new marriage or new job unless you bury him for good through forgiveness! Forgiveness releases inner healing and stops the dogs of offense in their tracks.

> Forgiveness releases inner healing and stops the dogs of offense in their tracks.

As we have seen with Herod, offenses can affect your entire life. Yet your future does not hinge on what is done to you, but on your *response* to those things. In fact, response is everything! In the chapters that follow we are going to chain the dogs, bury the ghosts and get on with living. Ready? Let's go!

Follow-up Questions

1. Are you haunted by ghosts from relationships past? Who are they?
2. Is it difficult for you to step into a new job or other key relationships because all you see is "John"? Does "John" seem to follow you everywhere you go?
3. Is "John" affecting any current relationships in your life? How and with whom?

I encourage you to courageously face the "Johns" of your life and give them to God. A good first step would be to walk courageously into the next chapters.

Part 3

Response Is Everything!

When they hurled their insults at him, he did not retaliate; when he suffered, he made no threats.

1 Peter 2:23, NIV

10

Things That Do Not Fix It

People with unresolved offenses do some of the things they do for two reasons: the *stated* reason and the *real* reason. Instead of being truthful, facing the hurt and dealing with it, they choose other routes that only worsen the situation and give the devil a foothold. Their true feelings emerge later when the damage already has been done. Experience brings to mind a few examples.

If You Can't Beat 'Em, Demonize 'Em

"Sue?" a deeply concerned sister Jane says on the phone. "I'm not calling to gossip, I just wanted to get you to pray about something. Did you know that brother

Bill has a major temper problem? Why, just yesterday he exploded at me in the choir room over absolutely nothing. I was stunned! I have since learned that he has had this problem for years and hasn't done a thing about it! I'm *so grieved* over it. I'm calling because I just knew you would want to pray for him."

"Oh, I will!" replies Sue. "You say he exploded? Why, that's terrible! You know, he has always struck me as being a little strange. You remember that bruise on his wife's arm last week? I don't want to suggest anything, but I got the funniest feeling about it, as if she was trying to hide something."

"Oh, you don't think!" gasps Jane. "Well, something just has to be wrong. Maybe we should suggest to the choir director that he be removed for a season until all this is settled!"

> Someone once remarked that the church has a grapevine Ernest and Julio Gallo would envy.

An affirming Sue replies, "It's the least we could do for the choir. We don't want the Spirit grieved. I'll call a couple of the other ladies and get them to pray as well. Why don't you tell the choir director?"

"I'd be glad to," replies Jane, who hangs up with a slight smile on her face. "Bill should never have yelled at me that way," she thinks to herself.

I think you see where I am going with this story. Someone once remarked that the church has a grapevine Ernest and Julio Gallo would envy. Have you ever noticed that we Christians do not gossip, but we share "prayer burdens"? We don't judge; we "discern." Christians carrying around unresolved offenses retaliate under the facade of being "grieved." We engage in different levels

94

of character assassination by "sharing" that "grief" with others. This is wrong, and Paul said so. "Be eager and strive earnestly to guard and keep the harmony and one-ness of [produced by] the Spirit in the binding power of peace" (Ephesians 4:3, AMPLIFIED).

Be eager. Strive earnestly. Christians are supposed to guard church unity as they would a safe full of their own money. But is that the attitude usually taken when people get hurt in the church?

Trojan Horse Tactics

I am reminded of what happened when the crafty Greeks entered the city of Troy in the mythological story. Unable to capture the city, they constructed a large wooden horse and secretly filled it with soldiers. Then they convinced the Trojans that its presence would make them invulnerable to attack, and the Trojans carried it through the city gates. Once inside, they opened the trap door, soldiers flooded into the streets and they won the war. In short, there was more to the eye than what the Trojans saw. A seemingly harmless object harbored an enemy.

> With the offended, many "Trojan horses" are employed to conceal true feelings.

With the offended, many "Trojan horses" are employed to conceal true feelings. For instance, the real issue with our "concerned" sister Jane was not concern at all. Bill had offended her, and she did not resolve her offense in a biblical way. Instead, she hid the offense in the Trojan horse of Christian concern, all the while demonizing him.

The Real Pros

The Pharisees and Sadducees were experts at Trojan horse tactics. Jesus and John the Baptist both experienced the sharp stab of their demonizing skills. Jesus commented on their methods with John when He said, "For John the Baptist came neither eating bread nor drinking wine, and you say, 'He has a demon'" (Luke 7:33).

Did they really believe this? No! The people believed John was a prophet, so they could not openly attack him. Instead, they crawled into the Trojan horse of spirituality, claiming "discernment," and demonized him.

Next they went for Jesus, who confronted them with their demonizing tactics by saying, "The Son of Man has come eating and drinking, and you say, 'Look, a glutton and a winebibber, a friend of tax collectors and sinners!'" (Luke 7:34).

What was the real issue with these Trojan horse pros? Why were they demonizing John and Jesus? The Pharisees, lawyers and other critics did not believe that John had a demon or that Jesus was a drunkard. The real reason they harshly criticized them is that they were offended by what their preaching required. Take John, for instance. "But the Pharisees and lawyers rejected the will of God for themselves, not having been baptized by him" (Luke 7:30).

The Pharisees and lawyers were offended. They did not want God's will and resented John's preaching. But they could not let the people know this because Jesus had declared John to be greater than a prophet (a highly respected office in Israel). So they rode a Trojan horse into the crowds by putting on a self-righteous spiritual mask and crying, "He has a demon!" Their philosophy was: If you can't beat 'em, demonize 'em.

Demonizing another is a classic Trojan horse tactic to hide one's own refusal to handle an offense in a scriptural way. The Pharisees used the same demonizing ploy with Jesus by accusing Him of being a drunkard and glutton. Once they demonized Him, they could justify rejecting Him. Deep down they knew better. It has been said that moral indignation is often jealousy with a halo. This was certainly the case with the Pharisees, lawyers and Sadducees of whom the Bible records, "For He knew that they had handed Him over because of envy" (Matthew 27:18).

> Demonizing another is a classic Trojan horse tactic to hide one's own refusal to handle an offense in a scriptural way.

Offended people often play the same Trojan horse game of demonizing the character of their offender while hiding behind a spiritual mask of innocence. The truth usually comes out when the horse has made it past the gates and the enemy wreaks havoc in the city.

I Am Not Offended, Just Hurt

Years ago an acquaintance of mine was sitting on stage as a featured conference speaker. He had the flu and felt horrible. When a friend sitting next to him asked if he felt all right, he responded, "Oh, I feel great!" After some minutes the friend blurted, "Why don't you admit that you're sick so the Lord can heal you!" Good advice. If we do not admit the truth, we cannot receive healing when we need it most.

The "I'm not offended, just hurt" response only temporarily relieves the offended person from facing reality. It does not make sense to say that you are hurt but not offended. Offense and hurt are

> When we deny an offense, we only postpone the inevitable.

siblings. Hurt is the result of being offended. Offenses cause pain, and if the hurt is not healed the trap of Satan will spring. By the time you realize what has happened, you have followed the bread trail under the box.

Everyone Jesus healed in the Bible admitted his or her infirmity, even if it caused embarrassment—as in the case of the woman with the issue of blood. Offenses work the same way. We must admit the offense and face up to it before healing can begin.

When we deny an offense, we only postpone the inevitable. Those who practice living in denial start believing their own deception. Here is a good way to remember where denial leads:

Don't
Even
KNow
It's
A
Lie

If you deny something long enough, you will start to believe the lie. Healing comes only when you confess the truth. "Confess your trespasses to one another, and pray for one another, that you may be healed" (James 5:16).

To derail an offense, we must *get it out*. Put your cards on the table. As the old song said, "You gotta know when to hold 'em, know when to fold 'em." With offenses, never "hold 'em." Like steam in a teapot, offense slowly rises to the top, and the whistle blows when it reaches the boiling point. But confession chains the dogs of offense and silences their howling.

I Feel "Led" Elsewhere

Let's talk about church attendance for a moment. All too many pastors and church leaders know the "I feel led elsewhere" statement. Does God lead His children? Yes. Does He lead them to run from offenses? *No*. But Christians leave their church homes and other crucial relationships at the slightest provocation instead of staying and working through the issues of an offense. Floating from church to church, they blame God for their wishy-washiness by saying they are "led" when, in fact, they often are reacting to an offense. The maddening "revolving back door" is turned by unresolved offenses that could have been settled easily.

It is a familiar pattern. The departing say they are not offended yet leave without saying goodbye to leadership and friends. When encountered in the mall they do not speak. If cornered, they paint on that unmistakable smile that looks as if it might crack under the pressure of a forced grin. They often bad-mouth their former church and call old church friends to come where it is "really happening." Healing is forfeited when offenses are handled this way, and discord is sown where peace should be. The wounds just keep getting deeper.

Stay-ability

God indeed may lead us to new places of fellowship, but so do offenses. Scripture introduces us to a God of commitment and covenant. He does not lead us from place to place like restaurant hoppers, eating here one week and there the next. Rather, God teaches us to work through painful issues, not run from them. He encourages "stay-ability" by giving us the "ability to stay." David declared, "Those who are planted in the house of the LORD shall flourish in the courts of our God" (Psalms 92:13).

You might say, "But Jeff, I am blessed anywhere I go!" That is true; you are blessed in Jesus. But God plants His people. The people He places around us, the circumstances in which He puts us and the challenges He allows to come our way all are designed to perfect His divine plan. When God is ready to move you, He will release you. *You will know it.* Great peace will accompany His guidance. It will be as Isaiah described: "For you shall go out with joy, and be led out with peace" (Isaiah 55:12). Out with joy, not anger. Led by peace, not offense!

Yet now, more than any time in recent history, people are more nomadic in their church attendance and other major commitments. This is because we have come to view church as a temporary fix for our problems instead of a long-term home where we enjoy deep, lasting relationships. As soon as our "needs" are not met or we become offended, we look elsewhere.

In his insightful book *The Second Coming of the Church,* George Barna discovered the following: "More and more Americans are beginning to view churches

100

as a 'rest stop' along their spiritual journey, rather than as their final destination." He cites four factors: our transience as a society, our preference for variety in church experiences, our perception that spiritual growth comes from discovery rather than commitment and our changed perception that religion is a commodity that we consume, not one in which we invest. I would add one more to the list: Christians regularly are driven from church to church by unresolved offenses.

> Christians regularly are driven from church to church by unresolved offenses.

Recently I was speaking with a senior citizen who has been a Christian for only a few years. She told me that one of the most discouraging things to her newfound faith was the constant changeover in her church's membership. "It really makes Christianity look bad to the lost," she said. What she really was saying was that it made Christianity look bad to her. People who change churches because they are offended will never enjoy the blessing God intended.

In his book *The Bait of Satan,* John Bevere describes the development of what he calls a "spiritual vagabond":

Once you leave the place God has chosen for you, your root system begins to dwarf. The next time it will be easier for you to flee from adversity because you have been careful not to root yourself deeply. You end up coming to the place where you have little or no strength to endure hardship or persecution.

You then become a spiritual vagabond, wandering from place to place, suspicious and afraid that others will mistreat you. Crippled and hindered in your ability to produce true spiritual fruit, you struggle in a self-centered life, eating the remains of the fruit of others.

101

I once was told of someone who said of her former church, "I just left quietly." But she left offended, and that cannot be done quietly. It gets out. When one leaves a church offended, it immediately affects at least five to ten others. Anyone who has been in a congregation for any length of time has become known, made connections and friendships and, contrary to what he or she says, cannot leave quietly. Leaving offended creates a wound within the body, leaving unanswered questions, suspicion toward leadership and a bad taste in the mouth of those who loved the person. In short, leaving offended is not the Jesus way.

Ever the Victim

"It's not my fault" has become the mantra of our day. Our culture is sick with the "victim" complex. Nobody is guilty, owns up to anything or does anything wrong—or so they say. If you do wrong, it is because the first wrong was done to you. It is an exercise in futility to try to correct because, no matter what, the person did not do it! It is someone else's fault, right down to blaming genetics for wrong choices.

This outlook destroys the chances of dealing with offenses. The blame game is sort of like that Trojan horse: You hide from your offense by demonizing another. It solves nothing. As long as you blame someone else for your problems you will never be healed or grow up. If people offended you, they were wrong. But if you continue to carry the offense, you are wrong.

Joseph, David, Paul and countless others bore the sharp edge of unfair criticism and persecution. They could have grabbed a violin, pointed to their offenders

102

and blamed them for all their ills. But they did not. They forgave, turned their enemies over to God and moved on to make their mark. So must we!

We have seen some of the wrong ways to respond to offenses, but what is the Jesus way? How do you successfully navigate through offenses and emerge victorious, staying truly free from the death-grip of bitterness? There *is* an answer.

Follow-up Questions

1. Do you recognize any of the above from personal experience? Which ones?
2. Are you nurturing any of them right now?
3. Is there an offense issue in your life about which you may be in denial?

I encourage you to courageously take bold steps toward handling your offense the Jesus way (covered in the next few chapters).

11

Choices

I t is not *what* happens to you that is most important. It is *how you respond* to what happens that matters most. Our response to offenses is what determines their power, not the offense itself.

An old castle in England bears the following inscription:

THEY SAY.

WHAT DO THEY SAY?

LET THEM SAY.

This inscription is great advice because it expresses a freedom. You cannot become the victim of an offense unless you allow it. You cannot control what others say or do, but you can respond in a way that keeps you free of offense. The key to overcoming offenses is the right response.

No one can make you blow your stack, spiral into depression or grab a violin and throw a pity party. If you decide to "get even" or rake someone over the hot coals of your seething temper, it is *your* choice. You might say, "My emotions just get the better of me!" But the Bible teaches that you should get the better of your emotions! "As, therefore, God's picked representatives, purified and beloved, put on that nature which is merciful in action, kindly in heart and humble in mind" (Colossians 3:12, PME).

> The key to overcoming offenses is the right response.

We are to "put on" the right response just as we choose what we will wear in the morning. In fact, all believers should get dressed twice each day—once in clothes and the other in Christ. The commands to "put on" and "put off" are found repeatedly in the New Testament. We are to "put on" Christ, "put on" love and "put off" the old man with its evil deeds (see Ephesians 4:22, 24). Believe me, the right response is not something that puts you in a headlock and makes you submit to it. You have to put it on by faith!

Attitude, Attitude, How Does Your Garden Grow?

Our responses to adversity, in turn, shape and mold that little eight-letter word—*attitude*. Our attitudes are not shaped by what happens to us. Rather, attitude is shaped by how we *respond* to what happens. Attitude is the result of responses, not events.

Show me someone with a chip on his or her shoulder, and I will show you someone who has responded negatively to adversity. Likewise, show me someone with a winning attitude, and I will show you someone who chose to respond positively time and again in trying times. We are not victims of circumstances but *products* of responses to circumstances. Responses to adversity are the bricks that build the house of attitude, and attitude decides the quality of one's life.

No one develops an angry, defeated or pessimistic attitude overnight. A person's attitude is the sum total of a thousand minor and major responses to adversity. Why does this matter with offenses? As a door swings on hinges, the outcome of offense swings on one's response to it, either opening the person to new opportunities or shutting him out of them. What has hurt and offended a person is not what will shape him, but one's response to it will.

It has been said that the same sun that melts butter hardens clay. That is also true of people. Under trials, one person becomes bitter, while another becomes better. But neither genetics nor circumstances determine who will do one or the other. It is a decision. In a storm at sea, the captain cannot control the direction the wind blows, but he *can* control the direction of the rudder. Responses, big and small, are up to us. We hold the wheel that turns the rudder of the ship!

> Responses, big and small, are up to us. We hold the wheel that turns the rudder of the ship!

Attitude, like good health, decides one's quality of life. Show me a negative, pessimistic person who is happy, and I will show you a frog that flies. It just does not work that way! Some are able to learn from tough experiences, to choose positive responses instead of angry reactions and move on. Others become bitter and reactionary by choice. Stuck in a time warp, they cannot move into the brightness of the future because they have chosen to sulk in the shadows of the past.

The Man in the Park

In 1973 what the press dubbed the "Jesus movement" was sweeping the world like a forceful, refreshing breeze. Jesus was actually popular in America! For some time, I had desired to hold an outdoor evangelistic meeting, and this beautiful Saturday evening in Dallas with spring's magic touch seemed the perfect time. I was excited. Expectation filled the air like an electric current. As we put together our little makeshift stage in a local park, curious people strolling through stopped and stared, wondering what we were doing.

As the speaker, I was experiencing those familiar butterflies that I felt whenever anticipating facing a new crowd. While the musicians tuned their guitars, I decided to walk toward a little snow-cone booth I had spotted earlier. That is when I met Joe.

"Whatcha doin'?" Joe asked with a smile on his face as he casually approached me. I guessed him to be around sixty with gray, thinning hair, a slightly stooped back and cautious, darting eyes. I introduced myself, shook his hand and told him we were there to hold an evangelistic service. He seemed to like that, so much so that he bought me a snow cone.

"Thanks!" I said with a smile.

We began to chat and, as talks usually go, I asked him about his background. All was fine until the subject turned to church. "Are you actively attending any-where?" I asked. A dark cloud suddenly covered his face. His brows furrowed, and his brown eyes began to smolder. In a New York second I sensed I had entered a minefield. But it was too late to turn back. As the band continued to warm up and the quiet dusk fell around us, I listened to Joe's story, like it or not.

Joe had been a committed member of a well-known, long-standing church in the community and loved it. There every time the doors opened, he did all he could to help make it a success. He had been involved in several groups and knew many of the members well. If something needed to be done, no matter how lowly, Joe was there. Church was his home away from home—that is, until the incident.

As he recounted his story, his face grew even darker. I could see his mind reliving events as if he were watching a movie. *Visualization.* No longer in the park, he had triggered the rewind button and clearly was far away, back to a place of great pain.

Joe and the pastor had a falling out—a bad one. Two apparently stubborn men had locked horns over a fairly small matter, and neither would give in. In a moment of supreme immaturity their conflict came to physical blows. Insult led to injury. Threats and counter-threats flew. Joe, reeling from hurt and rage, stomped out of the building, never to return.

As I listened to his sad tale, I began to formulate a plan. Surely the two could be persuaded to meet and talk it through. After all, I thought, the pastor has got to be hurting over this as much as Joe is. I would even be willing to go with him and act as a peacemaker! Enthusiastically, I suggested my plan, but Joe's countenance grew even darker. "I'll never return to that church!" he growled. "Besides, I don't even know if the pastor is still alive."

Taken back, I asked him if the pastor was ill. He said he was not certain, as it had been so long ago. Sensing even deeper waters, I asked Joe how long it had been. He looked at me with an expression I remember vividly to this day and spat out, "Why, 24 years!"

I was shaken to a cold reality. Before me stood a man who had lost 24 years of life, love, fellowship and spiritual potential. Offense had led him, step by step, under that fateful box of bitterness. He was a poster boy for the familiar pattern: indignation, justification, visualization and actualization. Only God knows what Joe's life could have been. I shook his hand, told him I would pray for him and headed to the stage. Not surprisingly, I did not see him in the crowd that night.

Like Joe, offended people exist in a snapshot, a still frame of time. A painful slice of life becomes a controlling tyrant, ruling their emotions from events long gone. They live in yesterday, not today—and they certainly do not look toward a bright tomorrow.

God told Lot's wife not to look back toward Sodom. But she did and became a pillar of salt—frozen, unable to move on, a metaphor of the person whose focus is backward, not forward. A divided focus always produces a paralyzed life.

You may have never moved past a nasty divorce, a bad business deal or the betrayal of a friend. If so, you are frozen in time. When you talk to others, it takes mere moments before the past comes pouring out again. Everyone else has moved on but you. Please believe me, nothing you have suffered through yesterday is worth losing today and all your tomorrows!

A great little statement I heard some time ago stuck in my mind and often speaks to me when I experience an offense: There is a reason the windshield is bigger than the rearview mirror! Simple, yet so true. You cannot drive a car while looking in the rearview mirror without crashing into something. The rearview mirror is for occasional glances, not total focus. Life is the same way. We gain perspective from the past. We hope to learn from past mistakes. But we cannot live in the past and build a future. You might pitch a tent in the past, but never build a house there. Let your stay be brief. The past is called the past for a reason—*it has passed!*

> There is a reason the windshield is bigger than the rearview mirror!

Forget It!

Paul was a man with a past, both good and bad. The good included a brilliant scholastic upbringing and accomplishments far beyond his peers. The bad was headlined by the persecution and murder of Christians—even though he actually thought he was doing a service for God. Paul had much to overcome. We can learn from him not to let past mistakes obscure a brilliant future. He said, "Forgetting what is behind and straining toward what is ahead" (Philippians 3:13–14, NIV).

Forgetting is taken from a word meaning "to lose out of mind." If you do not "lose out of your mind" some things, you might end up "losing your mind" because of them. You must choose to discard some memories. It is like taking out the trash. Why do you do it? It stinks, and it serves no purpose! It is your choice to "put out"

110

some things that need to go out. No one can make you do it. You must choose to do it for yourself. You can move forward into the future, but you cannot go back into the past. Do not waste time and energy on things that you no longer can do anything about. Forget it!

A Lesson from a Dog

I have a friend who owns a beautiful Labrador retriever that loves to catch Frisbees. Every time I visit, I look forward to watching Honeybee chase down my hardest throws—always catching the Frisbee in mid-air. She is poetry in motion. Honeybee loves walking proudly back to me, Frisbee firmly in mouth as if to say, "There is nothing you can throw that I can't catch!"

One evening after watching her make a particularly spectacular catch, a thought struck me. *What would she do if I threw another Frisbee while the first one was still in her mouth?* Smiling mischievously, I threw a second one long and hard. I will never forget the look on that dog's face when the second Frisbee sailed over her head just as she was halfway back with the first one. If a dog could go cross-eyed, she did! She looked up, looked at me, looked up again and made the decision. Dropping the first Frisbee, she chased the second one down, caught it in mid-air, walked back to the first one, picked it up and trotted back to me with both of them in her mouth. I was rolling with laughter! Only later did a thought hit me: *Even a dog was able to make the decision to let go of something old in order to catch something new!*

Is there a Frisbee headed toward you that requires letting go? Can you drop an offense to catch something new? To successfully let go of your pain, you must learn *what not to do* when the dogs of offense attack. There are several common reactions to offense that only make matters worse. Let's cover a few of them before looking at the one way that really works.

Follow-up Questions

1. What responses have you chosen when faced with an offense? Were they good ones? How so?
2. If your attitude were a flavor, what would it be? Sweet? Bitter? Somewhere in between? What would those closest to you say?
3. What do you suspect God may be telling you to forget or drop?

I encourage you to obey the still, small voice within. Anything He is telling you to deal with is for your ultimate good. Trust it!

12

Shake It Off!

In Acts 28 we read of Paul being shipwrecked on an island called Malta, which happened to be inhabited by friendly natives who built a fire for Paul and those with him to warm themselves. As Paul was gathering sticks to stoke the flames, a highly venomous serpent suddenly lunged from the bundle and fastened itself onto Paul's hand. The natives immediately assumed that he was evil and the "gods" were punishing him. Yet it says, "But he shook off the creature into the fire and suffered no harm" (verse 5).

This snake was probably what is called a "two-stepper," common to that part of the world. They call it this because after it bites a person he or she takes about two steps and is dead. Yet Paul was unharmed. He "shook off" what could have killed him by his strong faith in Christ. In the same way, we can "shake off" venomous offenses into the fire of Christ's love before becoming poisoned.

The "Teflon" Response

You may remember when the new "Teflon" pans came out. They were touted as "no muss, no fuss" utensils. The pitch was that nothing stuck to them. I recall a TV commercial that showed a fried egg sliding right out of one of them without any cooking oil. Teflon changed pans forever!

> Like Paul and the serpent, we can shake off offenses into the fire and remain unharmed.

Likewise, Jesus knew the deadly potential of offenses and taught us how to respond to them in a way that would keep them from sticking. I call it the "Teflon response" to an offense. This is the response of choice because it spares us from longer-term repercussions. Like Paul and the serpent, we can shake off offenses into the fire and remain unharmed.

The Teflon response worked for me! Do not miss the epilogue, where I will finish the story of that ten thousand dollar theft that I began in chapter 1.

How It Works

After reminding His listeners of their Old Testament belief that they should love their neighbors but hate their enemies, Jesus introduced a whole new concept: "But I say to you, love your enemies" (Matthew 5:44). The first thing that strikes us about the command to love our enemies is that Jesus focused on response, not on the offense itself.

The best of us would admit that loving enemies is not easy. In fact, loving an enemy is a divine, supernatural act that is impossible without the grace of God! But it is also a choice that God empowers us to make. Our response to an offender decides how we ultimately will come through it. So let's talk about the rules of response.

> The first thing that strikes us about the command to love our enemies is that Jesus focused on response, not on the offense itself.

Response Rule #1: Be pre-emptive. Decide beforehand what your response to offenses will be. Jesus is not suggesting that we pray about loving our enemies—He commands us to do it. "I say to you" translates *non-negotiable!* This is how we are to walk in the Kingdom of God. The best approach is to be ready, because offenses will come—guaranteed. A policeman does not decide whether or not to carry a gun when he encounters a criminal; he already has it. The worst time to decide what to put in the offering plate is when the plate is two people away from you. Likewise, the worst time to decide your response to an offense is *after* you are offended.

Response Rule #2: Be quick. Respond immediately the way Christ taught. If you sit and stew over a wrong, you are going to lose the battle. The offense will find its mark and stick. The Teflon response requires a swift decision, before negative emotions gain a foothold. Jesus said, "Come to terms quickly with your enemy before it is too late" (Matthew 5:25, TLB). No stranger to offenses, Paul gave the same advice: "Don't let the sun go down with you still angry—get over it quickly; for when you are angry you give a mighty foothold to the devil" (Ephesians 4:26–27, TLB). Offenses have a 24-hour expiration date. After that they go sour.

Do not let the sun set with an offense simmering inside. Deal with it as quickly as you would remove a rattlesnake out of your living room. Satan gains a strategic advantage over us when we harbor offenses. *Foothold* means "ground" or "opportunity." Like a military general advancing on foreign land, Satan moves in quickly to take advantage of any hesitation. That is why Jesus taught the Teflon response!

> Offenses have a 24-hour expiration date. After that they go sour.

On the Offense with Offenses!

According to Jesus, enemies come in four categories—cursers, haters, users and persecutors, and they all bring offenses. For each type of offender, Jesus gave an "on the offense" response. Instead of leaving us in a victim position, He placed us squarely in a proactive position. In Matthew 5:44, He provides three Teflon responses guaranteed to keep the offense from sticking.

Teflon Response #1: "Bless those who curse you." The word *bless* is taken from the Greek word from which we get "eulogy." For instance, when someone is "eulogized" at a funeral, a person speaks well of him or her. Does this suggest that we should be disingenuous and say things about the "curser" that are not true? No. But we should refuse to be "devil-like."

The Greek word for devil is *diabolos (dee-ab'-ol-os)*, and it means "slanderer." John called Satan the "accuser of the brethren" (see Revelation 12:10). Satan is an accuser and a curser. When he speaks, it reeks of the condemnation of an accusing hell.

As children of God, we are forbidden to engage in "devil-talk," which is to accuse and call down curses on others. When our enemies curse us, they are the unwitting tools of Satan, and we are to refuse to get into the gutter with them. "And as for those who try to make your life a misery, bless them. Don't curse, bless" (Romans 12:14, PME). If you are in charge of your mouth, you are the one in charge!

> As children of God, we are forbidden to engage in "devil-talk," which is to accuse and call down curses on others.

Teflon Response #2: "Do good to those who hate you." Why should we do something good for someone who hates us? Because it keeps the offense from sticking, and it keeps our own hearts free! But there is another reason as well. Again Paul chimes in: "Dear friends, never avenge yourselves. . . . Instead, feed your enemy if he is hungry. If he is thirsty give him something to drink and you will be 'heaping coals of fire on his head'" (Romans 12:19, 20, TLB).

I believe God gives us opportunities to do good things for those who hate us. If your heart is right and you are on the lookout, He usually will allow you to see a need. The "hater" may be going through problems with his or her children, a divorce or a job. Whatever it may be, the observant believer seeking to obey Scripture often will be allowed to see a need along with an opportunity to help. When we do good to our enemies, the hot coals of conviction fall on their heads. It can even prove to be the trigger that leads the person to Christ.

He goes on to tell us *why* this should be our response. "Don't let evil get the upper hand, but conquer evil by doing good" (verse 21). Responding scripturally breaks the power of evil.

Teflon Response #3: "Pray for those who spitefully use you and persecute you." You cannot remain angry or bitter at someone for whom you are praying. No doubt Jesus knew this, and that is why He told us to do it. Remember His prayer from the cross? Except for a few women, His bloodied gaze saw only enemies jeering at Him. Yet He prayed, "Father, forgive these people, for they do not know what they are doing" (Luke 23:34, TLB). It is hard to pray for people who intentionally are using or persecuting you, but a root of bitterness is harder to handle!

> It is hard to pray for people who intentionally are using or persecuting you, but a root of bitterness is harder to handle!

Throughout His life, Jesus modeled the Teflon response to a T. Listen to the moving way Peter describes His response to offenders: "Who, when He was reviled, did not revile in return; when He suffered, He did not threaten, but committed Himself to Him who judges righteously" (1 Peter 2:23). And Peter leaves no doubt that this should be our response to enemies: "For to this you were called, because Christ also suffered for us, leaving us an example, that you should follow His steps" (verse 21).

If we want to keep the offense from sticking, we are to be preemptive, respond quickly, bless, do good and pray for offending enemies. If you wait for the right emotions to sweep over you, you will wait in vain. Your emotions will take you down the bread trail every time.

You must make a firm decision to act on the Word of God.

But what do you do if you just cannot get past it? You have tried and tried, yet the anger remains. What now? Jesus anticipated this and told us exactly what to do.

Follow-up Questions

1. Are you faced right now with one of the enemies Jesus mentioned?
2. Do you still have time to practice the Teflon response?
3. What will happen if you do not? How will things be different if you do?

I encourage you to act quickly and respond according to Christ's teachings. You can do it!

_13_

When You Just Cannot
Get Past It

I n 1854, Asiatic cholera swept through London like the pale horseman of the Apocalypse. Thousands were swiftly wiped out, while bodies were ominously stacked on the sides of streets, waiting for horse-drawn carriages to take them away. The grim reaper was no respecter of persons, with young and old, rich and poor alike falling prey to the mysterious disease.

Even more debilitating was the sense of hopelessness over the unknown cause. Panic set in. Everything and everyone became suspect. Tragically, the dying often were neglected.

Around a year into the plague Dr. John Snow entered the sad scene. Snow suspected the plague was being transmitted by contaminated water. To prove his theory, he began observing a prominent water pump in a heavily trafficked area of downtown London on Broad Street. Carefully monitoring those stricken with cholera, he checked to see how many of them had also drunk from the suspicious pump. Snow soon discovered the death rate was far higher than anywhere else in the city. Eureka!

Acting quickly, he ordered the pump removed from the well. Like a dark, receding cloud the plague withdrew, losing its deadly momentum. What could have been a far greater catastrophe lasted just one year. Amazingly, when just one inconspicuous pump was removed, London was healed!

The deadly fountain of bitterness is similar to the Broad Street pump. Most who watch the destruction caused by offenses do not understand the source or how to stop it. Jesus, however, knew all about the pump and carefully told us how to shut it down.

When You Are the One Offended

What do you do when the offense sticks? How do you untangle the gnarly roots of anger and bitterness from your heart? You missed the Teflon response, so now what? One of my favorite sayings is, "When all else fails, follow directions." Then what are the directions for shutting the bitterness pump down? Jesus said, "Moreover if your brother sins against you, go and tell him his fault between you and him alone. If he hears you, you have gained your brother" (Matthew 18:15).

Jesus taught *confrontation*. That immediately becomes a bit distasteful to me, sort of like spiritual castor oil. I do not like confrontation, and I am sure you do not either. It is so much easier to hang back in the shadows and resort to the things mentioned in chapter 10 that do not really fix it. But if Jesus taught us to confront, He will give us the grace to do it. If you cannot get past it, the only way to pluck up the root of an offense is to confront the offender.

> **If you cannot get past it, the only way to pluck up the root of an offense is to confront the offender.**

Returning to Matthew 18:15, notice who is *not* involved in the first step—*anyone who is not directly part of the offense.* Jesus kept the issue between the offended and the offender. There are always people with whom we can share the stuff that really hurts, such as a best friend or spouse, but only if it will help you handle it better, and only if he or she is mature and will not take up a grudge on your behalf.

The bottom line is—if at all possible, it is best to go directly to the offender. Going to others may allow you to vent, but it does not solve the problem. Jesus said to go to the person who offended you and *tell him his fault.* But a word of caution is in line: Confrontation requires wisdom, or you may end up in an even stickier situation. Here are a few words of advice before you confront an offender.

Confrontation Rule #1: Pray Before You Go

Urban legend has it that scientists at NASA developed a gun to launch dead chickens at the windshields of airplanes, military jets and space shuttles at a speed that closely matches maximum velocity. In order to test windshield strength, this curious invention simulates collisions that frequently occur with airborne fowl. British engineers heard about the gun and were eager to test it on their high-speed trains.

They made the necessary arrangements and were shocked at the result. The chicken hurtled out of the barrel, crashed into the shatterproof windshield, smashed it into smithereens, crashed through the control console, snapped the engineer's backrest in two and embedded itself in the back wall of the cabin. The horrified Brits sent NASA the disastrous results, gave them the windshield schematics and begged the U.S. scientists for suggestions. NASA responded with one sentence: "Thaw the chicken."

Before you go charging off to your offender, *thaw the chicken*. You can do more damage than good if you go to the offender seething with anger. And most importantly, pray. Prayer settles the heart, calms the emotions and gives you time to gather your thoughts.

> Prayer settles the heart, calms the emotions and gives you time to gather your thoughts.

In her insightful and humorous book *Stick a Geranium in Your Hat and Be Happy*, Barbara Johnson said, "Disturbing things will remain disturbing as long as you are disturbed. But when you become peaceful, conditions will iron themselves out. Remember: Upset minds upset; peaceful minds 'peacefulize.'"

Pray also that God will show you anything *you* might have done to contribute to the situation. When we are offended, it is easy to see the faults of others. Allow God to walk you through the circumstances that led to the offense and reveal any part that you may have played.

Confrontation Rule #2: Prepare What You Want to Say and How to Say It

Wording is crucial. Someone once remarked that frankness does not require being brutal. That is true, and neither does confrontation. When confronting, wear a velvet glove. It does not have to be a shredding experience. The book of Proverbs advises, "The heart of the righteous studies how to answer" (Proverbs 15:28). Since wording is so important, here are a few suggestions to consider.

Remove accusing language. Angry accusation sabotages an attempt to bring reconciliation because it immediately places the alleged offender on the defensive. The imaginary exchange below will help to illustrate.

"John," an angry friend snaps, "someone told me they overheard you saying that I stole money from my business and that is why I got fired. How could you say such a thing!"

This attempt at confrontation is dead in the water because John is accused before he is even given a chance to give his side. It would be wiser to word it like this:

"John," a friend says in a calm voice, "I've been told that you were overheard saying I stole money from my business and that is why I got fired. *Is this what you said?*"

The second example removes accusation because it allows the alleged offender a chance to respond. When you calmly ask if something is true, the accused knows you have not believed what you have been told until you give him a chance to tell his side.

Do not interrupt. Interruption says to the offender that you really are not listening. It also communicates

124

that your mind is made up. The offender will already be on edge since you are confronting him, so relax and give him time to speak. He deserves to be heard just as much as you do.

Repeat what you understand him to be saying. Misunderstanding is the fuel that keeps the fire of offense roaring. For instance, in our above illustration the offender may respond by saying: "I did not say that you stole the money. I said that your business had turned up with money missing and that everyone was a suspect. It just happened to come on the tail end of your firing being discussed. But I didn't connect your name with the missing money."

> More times than not, offenses spring from what we think happened, not from what actually took place.

To be sure you get it, you reply: "Now let me be sure I understand. A discussion about the missing money took place minutes after my jobless situation came up. But when you made your statement about the money you were not linking it to me?"

He then replies, "Yes, and I apologize that it sounded otherwise."

I cannot tell you how often I have seen offenses created because words were pulled out of context and misconstrued! More times than not, offenses spring from what we think happened, not from what actually took place. This is why Scripture warns, "He who answers a matter before he hears it, it is folly and shame to him" (Proverbs 18:13).

My heart breaks at the great relationships I have seen ruined due to one side of a story being told before the alleged offender can give his or her side.

Wise confrontation stops the lies, embellishments and exaggerations that occur when offenses are left to run their course.

Keep the decibel level down. Those who study body language say that when dealing with angry people, it is best to sit in a relaxed position with legs crossed, hands down, and talk in a soft tone. In other words, promote peace by non-reactionary body language and soft volume. Remember, as the decibel level rises, communication sinks.

"The beginning of strife is like releasing water; therefore stop contention before a quarrel starts" (Proverbs 17:14). Raising your voice is like turning on a faucet. As it rises, you are turning the handle up on anger and the flow intensifies—like gushing water. When voices rise, communication escalates into a full-blown quarrel. Once screaming enters the picture, forget it! Have you ever noticed that at the scream level you usually lose track of what you were discussing in the first place? The whole thing sinks into a "he said, she said" blame game. "A soft answer turns away wrath, but a harsh word stirs up anger" (Proverbs 15:1).

Confrontation Rule #3: If Your Offense Is Based on Truth, Express Honestly How It Hurt You

Once you have determined that the offense is based on fact, it is time to lovingly tell the truth about how it hurt you. The fruits of loving confrontation are worth the risk. Jesus said: "If he hears you, you have gained your brother" (Matthew 18:15). Most reasonable people will respond to wise confrontation. If the confrontation is successful, you have salvaged a relationship!

Sometimes we cannot imagine facing our offender, or else, due to distance or other factors, a meeting is physically impossible. In this instance you may want to consider writing a letter or sending an e-mail. I have written both good and bad letters and have learned that the same principles listed above must apply. I strongly suggest you run your letter by a spiritually mature person (more on that in the next chapter) who can spot any inflammatory or unwise language. A good letter has the power to melt anger and resentment, paving the way for a personal meeting (if that is possible).

A powerful example is a little letter tucked away between Titus and Hebrews called Philemon. It is a masterpiece of letter-writing gauged to remove offense. Paul is writing to an offended Christian man whose slave Onesimus has fled from him. I strongly urge you to read this letter. Study carefully how Paul talks to Philemon, compliments him, appeals to his Christian senses and speaks lovingly to him, paving the way for the slave to return.

If you write a letter, the offended or offender will usually write back, opening the door to settle the issue. An offense can be beautifully handled by wise correspondence.

But what if he or she does not receive your attempts to reconcile? What then?

Follow-up Questions

1. Do you need to lovingly confront someone? If so, how do you think he or she will respond?
2. Have you thought through your approach? Your wording?

3. Have you prayed before going? Are you calmed?
4. Do you need to write a letter? Is your offender too far away to meet with? Go ahead and begin!

I encourage you to follow Jesus' instructions before hearts grow hard and the way is more difficult. A blessing awaits!

14

Bringing In Witnesses

W hen young David became king of Israel, a strong resistance from the fading house of Saul, led by a man named Abner, rose against him (see 2 Samuel 2:12). In a minor skirmish, Abner killed a fellow named Asahel, who just happened to be the brother of Joab, the captain of David's army. Abner did not want to do it, but Asahel refused to stop chasing Abner and forced the issue to a deadly conclusion.

As the conflict between the two kingdoms marched toward a close, Abner decided to align himself with King David. Yet before he could do so, Joab murdered him in cold blood. David was so disturbed by the act that he said, "And these men, the sons of Zeruiah, are too harsh for me" (2 Samuel 3:39).

David could not believe that his top general murdered a man who was on the verge of bringing the grievous conflict to an end. So he described Joab as being "too harsh for me." In your attempts to reconcile, you may encounter people who will likewise be harsh and un-cooperative.

> In your attempts to recon-cile, you may encounter people who will likewise be harsh and uncooperative.

As Joab's spirit differed from David's, the offender with whom you are dealing may be of a different spirit. Harsh and un-bending, he resists you and the teachings of Christ. In fact, if step one in the confrontation process has failed, it is probably for one of two reasons: The offense is real but the offender denies it, or the offender is unrepentant and unwilling to work it out biblically. It may be a stubborn Christian who refuses to take the steps given by Jesus, or a non-Christian who sees no use in it. Whatever the case, you are dealing with someone who has no heart for the process.

Paul apparently had run across a few of these in his time when he wrote, "If it is possible, as much as de-pends on you, live peaceably with all men" (Romans 12:18). In other words, not everyone will be agreeable to the reconciliation process. It will not always be pos-sible, no matter how hard you try. It is these types of people that test the mettle of our decision to confront and reconcile.

Sow It as a Seed

When you have done your best by investing time and energy to do the right thing and the effort seems wasted, know this—it is not! Their lack of response is beyond your control, but God will honor you if you refuse to get bitter and instead sow your effort as a seed of obedience for His glory. Do not allow yourself to develop a victim's attitude or to say it was not worth it. God is with you and will vindicate you! In doing the right thing your attempt at reconciliation was not a failure. They will answer for their lack of response, not you. Always remember that something powerful takes place when you do the *right thing,* no matter what others do.

For instance, I once tithed regularly into a ministry that I later found out had involved itself in misappropriation of funds and other financial abuses. My first response was to bewail the fact that I had "wasted" all that money because it had not gone toward what was promised. But one day God comforted my heart by assuring me that He saw my motive for the giving and would bless me, no matter what others had done. And He did indeed honor my sowing! I was not the victim of someone else's disobedience, and it is the same with sowing toward reconciliation.

When to Call Witnesses

If the offender is a Christian who is open to having others step in to mediate the situation, you may find it necessary to go to step two by bringing in witnesses. If they are not willing, however, it is highly unlikely much will be accomplished by taking this step.

Your authority to do this is found in the clear teaching of Jesus, who really tightened the screws in the event of an unsettled offense. "But if he will not hear, take with you one or two more, that 'by the mouth of two or three witnesses every word may be established'" (Matthew 18:16).

Generally speaking, the less people who are involved, the better. It is also vital that they be objective. Close

> An offense can be like an irritating gnat buzzing around your head or a devouring lion eating you alive.

friends or others who may be emotionally entangled through their attachment to you are not always the wisest choice.

Let me urge you at this juncture to take a hard look at how deep the river of offense really runs. Does your peace depend upon it? Is it affecting your ability to attend a particular church or to work at a particular job? Is it hindering your walk with God? An offense can be like an irritating gnat buzzing around your head or a devouring lion eating you alive.

Which is it? Because of the potential difficulties involved in this second step—if you can find it within you—it is best to take a deep breath, hold your head high, realize that you tried your best, sow your efforts as a seed for God to honor and move on.

Spiritual People

If you cannot get past the offense and are certain the issue must be taken to the second level (expressing openly in the presence of witnesses how you have been hurt), mediators should be chosen carefully. Paul gave the guidelines: "Brethren, if a man is overtaken in any trespass, you who are spiritual restore such a one in a spirit of gentleness, considering yourself lest you also be tempted" (Galatians 6:1).

Notice who Paul taps on the shoulder to be involved in restoration: *You who are spiritual.* Character, trustworthiness and maturity are the qualities of a good mediator. The following list may help in describing someone spiritual.

1. *His motivation is to restore, not expose.* "You who are spiritual restore. . . ." Spiritual people take no delight in the shortcomings of another and have no desire to expose and destroy someone who has been "overtaken" in a trespass.

2. *They will be under personal discipline.* "Considering yourself . . ." Spiritual people are submitted to the Lord and regularly examine their own spiritual lives. They work hard to stay right with God and to live a clean life. "But I discipline my body and bring it into subjection, lest, when I have preached to others, I myself should become disqualified" (1 Corinthians 9:27).

3. *They will judge with righteous judgment.* Righteous judgment does not take sides; it flows from love, is not mean spirited and has no personal agendas. Isaiah predicted that Jesus would judge in this manner: "He [Jesus] shall not judge by the sight of His eyes, nor decide by the hearing of His ears; but with righteousness He shall judge the poor, and decide with equity for the meek of the earth" (Isaiah 11:3–4).

4. *They will have a known track record with God.* Paul admonished, "And we urge you, brethren, to recognize those who labor among you" (1 Thessalonians 5:12). Spiritual people have a history with God as well as with His people. They are known in the congregation. Not fly-by-

133

nights, they have stuck with one fellowship long enough for others to observe their walk.

The purpose of the mediator is to affirm the reality of the offense and attempt to bring reconciliation between the two parties.

A Bad Day at the Office

Years ago as a young pastor I was called to a home where an explosion of emotions was taking place. The daughter of a church member had become pregnant out of wedlock. When I arrived and slowly walked through the front door it was like walking into a room filled with dynamite. The father, a huge, intimidating man, was sitting on the couch with the equivalent of radioactive steam coming out of his ears. His expression would have made an oak tree wilt. The mother was sitting across from him, afraid to say anything. The pregnant daughter was crying in the corner of the room, while her three other siblings, all teens, sat silently at the kitchen table. Gulp! Talk about needing words that seemed to be hiding from me!

The father, predictably, was the first to speak. He went on a tirade about the shame of it, how his daughter, raised in church, could have done such a thing, how he could "kill that boy" and so on. The daughter only began to cry harder while everyone else looked at me.

Just when I did not think the tension could get any worse, the pregnant daughter suddenly blurted, "But Dad, Mom was pregnant when ya'll got married!"

I looked at the front door to make sure it was not locked and to take stock of how fast I could get to it.

Befuddled and totally nonplussed by this statement of pure fact, the father muttered, "Well, someone should have killed me."

It was mediation time. They had been at it for days, and nothing was settled. Not wanting anyone to know, they realized that in a few short months the situation would become obvious. So they called me in as a peacemaker. It took a few hours, a calm voice, a non-accusatory attitude and a listening ear to do it, but by the time I left, the daughter and dad had cried and hugged, the mother sighed with relief, the siblings went softly to their rooms and a potential long-term nightmare of bitterness, vengeance and division was averted.

Mediation can be effective in troubled marriages, church division, spats between church members and other touchy scenarios. The mere presence of objective, calm brethren is a God-given incentive to be reasonable. According to Jesus, these mature believers also will serve as "witnesses" if the offender still refuses to respond to God, which leads us to the final step in Jesus' teaching.

Tell It to the Church

Since offenses rarely make it to this level, I will be brief. The third step in Jesus' instructions on handling offenses says, "And if he refuses to hear them, tell it to the church" (Matthew 18:17). This is not necessarily a command for the pastor to walk out on a Sunday morning, point out the offender and spill an offense to the entire congregation. Some offenses *do* need to be addressed on this level, as in the case of someone teaching damaging false doctrine to the congregation after clear warnings, but it is rare. The person involved would have had to totally resist the first two steps and defy local church authority. But wisdom is needed. Such a tactic could open the door to litigation, which no church wants.

Official church leadership comprising the senior and staff pastors can represent the "church" to which Jesus refers. The situation can be handled discreetly behind closed doors between the offender and church leadership.

In summary, if the offender will not hear the offended party or respect the affirmation of witnesses, the situation should be taken to top church leadership for final judgment. According to Christ, he can at this level be asked to leave the church if he refuses to repent.

When You Are the Offender

It is worth noting that Jesus left no stone unturned concerning offenses. In Matthew 5, He flips the coin and turns His focus on the person who knows he or she is the offender: "Therefore if you bring your gift to the altar, and there remember that your brother has something against you, leave your gift there before the altar, and go your way. First be reconciled to your brother, and then come and offer your gift" (Matthew 5:23–24).

These verses bring two words to mind: *urgency* and *priority*. Going to the altar to offer a gift represents the sacrifice of worship in God's house. Jesus was so strong on handling offenses that He prioritized being reconciled to an offended brother or sister before worshiping! In other words, as mentioned in earlier chapters, reconcile and do it quickly. The longer we wait to reconcile, the deeper attitudes settle. Anger festers and hearts harden until they are like castles built of iron. First go make it right—humbly confess what you did and ask for forgiveness—then go and worship God. When things are right horizontally (in our earthly relationships), then the vertical (our relationship with God) is enhanced.

I Will If He Will First!

If Jesus' teachings on handling offenses are so crystal clear, why are they so rarely obeyed? Pride is generally the rub. It goes something like this: The offended person protests, "I am the one who has been hurt! Why should I go to him? I will get things right when he comes to me!" In the other corner of the ring is the offender whose attitude is, "If she is bugged about something, let her come to me!" In essence, "I'll move if you move first!" Consequently, nobody wins and nothing gets settled.

Things would be so much easier if the offending party would take the initiative and make it right according to Jesus' teaching! The offended party would not have to go through the confrontation process, witnesses would not be needed and gossip would be stopped. Voilá! Success!

A Fight with the Wife

I have a pastor friend who told me about a fight he once had with his wife. It became one of those "you're wrong, I'm right," blame games where nothing was solved. It just so happened that he was to preach in another church that evening. When the time arrived and the disagreement was still boiling, he grabbed his Bible, huffed out the door and sped out of the driveway—all the while informing God that He really needed to convict his erring spouse.

He had not gotten very far down the road when the Lord touched his heart with a question. *Where are you going?* My friend self-righteously replied, "To preach!" To which the Lord responded, *If you do not call her before you get there and make it right, I will not be with you tonight.* After struggling along for several more miles he blurted, "But Lord, she was wrong, not me!" The Holy Spirit gently started bringing to mind the angry, destructive words he had spoken to her.

Sheepishly pulling into a gas station, he called from a payphone and muttered, "I'm sorry."

She said, "It's about time you called!" She knew as well as he did that he could not preach until it was settled. That night he spoke with great liberty!

If you have offended someone, do not come to God as if nothing were wrong. Take care of it! Reconcile with your friend or loved one, and then worship God with a clear conscience.

The hurt and pain brought on by offenses can be great. It is often a longer journey than anticipated when getting over the hurt and devastation. You can forgive, but God still has to heal the pain. Is there anything that can help anchor our souls and stiffen our resolve to see it through? Yes! We will call them *cave lights.*

Follow-up Questions

1. Are you dealing with someone unresponsive to reconciliation? If so, what steps are you going to take?
2. Is God giving you grace to lay it down and go on? Have you been successful?
3. If not, have you prayed for and sought out wise mediators?

I encourage you to move boldly in Jesus' way of handling the offense. He will honor it!

Part 4

Cave Lights

Because His compassions fail not. They are new every morning.

Lamentations 3:22–23

_15_

The Light of Wisdom

In his book *The Art Of War,* Sun-Tzu wrote:

> If you know the enemy and know yourself, you need not
> fear the result of a hundred battles. If you know your-
> self but not the enemy, for every victory gained you will
> also suffer a defeat. If you know neither the enemy nor
> yourself, you will succumb in every battle.

Likewise, in the arena of offenses we must know both
our enemy and ourselves. The best time to be armed
with wisdom for the tough battle through offense is
now, not while trying to wade through the raging river
of angry emotions and an aching heart. Wisdom is to
know yourself, your enemy and, I would add, the ways
of God.

Part 4 of this book is going to place the tools of hope and encouragement into your hands. It is dedicated to arming you with wisdom and comfort while you gain strength and restoration. Remember, to win the fight you must know yourself, your enemy and the ways of God.

A Flashlight in the Cave

As a teenager, I once traveled with a group of other teens through beautiful New Mexico. Chaperoned by two adult guides, we climbed a mountain and then headed back to civilization. That is when I spotted the mouth of a small cave. It looked unexplored and, being the adventurous type, I hastily grabbed a flashlight and crawled on my hands and knees through the small entrance. I remember one of the counselors strongly advising me to stop, but mischief reigned and I experienced some things I have never forgotten. In fact, what happened in that cave vividly illustrates the trap of bitterness.

Upon entering, what first struck me was how lonely I felt. Though all of my traveling companions were just outside, I felt strangely cut off from them. Alone and isolated, the tomb-like cave distanced all sense of companionship from me.

Out of curiosity I turned the flashlight off to see how dark it actually was. That did not last long. It was dark—profoundly so. I could have stayed all day without my eyes adjusting. The rocks had no cracks or openings to let in even a hint of light. Just the slimmest glimpse of sunshine would have been comforting, but its unnerving corridors were draped in black. *What if my flashlight went dead?* Quickly, I flicked it back on!

Crawling a bit further, the gnawing feeling of being lost grew. All sense of direction faded. I knew that to reach the cave's mouth I had to go backward, but I could not escape the frightening sense of being off course. Choking back panic, the questions started coming. Was what I remembered to be backward truly the way I had first entered? Had I made a turn and forgotten? Distinctions faded. Every wall looked the same.

That was when I realized I was not alone. As I shined my flashlight straight ahead, I heard a squeaking sound above me. Turning the light up, I was horrified by what I saw. The rock ceiling was covered with bats, hanging upside down as if they had all turned to see who had invaded their dark home. For a moment I froze. One sudden movement could have spooked them and filled the cave with flying, biting predators! Gathering my wits, I slowly began crawling backward on my hands and knees. I was never happier to see the cave's mouth again. It was such a relief to break out into the sunshine—leaving behind those creatures of the night.

> The only comfort I had in that dark, eerie cave was my flashlight.

The only comfort I had in that dark, eerie cave was my flashlight. Though seemingly insignificant now, that simple, ordinary flashlight served several key purposes. It guided me, revealed the dangers in the cave and brought me comfort.

It is the same in the cave of offense, which is similar to that New Mexico cave into which I crawled. For instance, when you are in a cave of offense you feel lonely and lost. Feelings of isolation set in while your clear

145

sense of direction and purpose slip away. And like the bats in the cave, unsavory creatures are there—depression, anger, fear and loneliness, just to name a few. If not for God's help we would become lost in our pain, fall prey to danger and lose all sense of peace. Reflecting on my cave experience, the adult guide was much like Jesus crying out to stop me before I crept into real danger. As we so often do when Jesus calls to us, I ignored him.

But I did get out—with the help of that flashlight! On your way out of offense, God lovingly places "flashlights" in your hand that both encourage and empower you to go through the valley to the other side. In the next few chapters we will consider four of them.

The Light of Wisdom Reveals the Benefit of Suffering

The first flashlight is wisdom, which is the knowledge of God and His ways. Only wisdom can help you see that God can use the suffering brought on by painful offense. The knowledge that pain will work for your benefit is one of the flashlights of encouragement that God sends into the cave of suffering. We may not like to hear it, but pain is one of life's best teachers. God wastes nothing in your life—not even pain.

> God wastes nothing in your life—not even pain.

Not that I look for pain. I have never had to do so. Pain has always managed to find me. In his book *The Seven Seasons of a Man's Life*, Patrick Morley observed, "We may suffer for one or more of three reasons:

146

1. For doing wrong
2. For doing right
3. For no apparent reason

How we respond to our suffering depends on why we are suffering in the first place."

If we are suffering for something we did wrong, we must forgive ourselves—as mentioned in chapter 7. If we are suffering for Christ's sake, we are encouraged to happily endure it. But we may be suffering for something we do not understand, which is the most difficult. Painful circumstances come, and we cannot connect the dots. Someone or something has hurt us, and it makes no sense.

We may never understand why bad things happen to good people, or why we suffer when we have done nothing wrong. For instance, I do not understand in my natural mind why God allows a hardened criminal to live a long life while a precious, loving saint with a husband and children dies of cancer at a young age. It is a mystery. But I do know this—God is the one who knows the *whys* of life, and we must learn to trust Him.

> Paul sounded the trumpet loud and clear—God wants us to know that He's going to work through every storm for our benefit!

Paul sounded the trumpet loud and clear—God wants us to know that He is going to work through every storm for our benefit! You probably know the verse, but chew slowly on the following eight words: "And we know that all things work together . . ." (Romans 8:28). *All things.* That is a lot of things! Let's consider a few: disappointment, disillusionment, discouragement, heartache, failures, mistakes, good times, bad times, in-between times, ups and downs, ins and outs, glad days, sad days, shocks, disasters, betrayals, and on it goes. In other words—life. Life happens, period. And sometimes it brings suffering. Yet the flashlight of God's wisdom lights the way before us and says: It is in knowing that it will be worked for your good that carries you to the other side.

Do you *know* deep down what the above verse is saying? If your answer is "yes," are you convinced that this divine principle is at work in your life? Do you believe that an all-powerful, sovereign God is able to take your pain and make it serve His ultimate purpose? You may never understand what possessed someone to hurt you, but can you still trust God to bring good from a bad experience?

Staying mad and sulking about an offense is like that dark, muddy cave. I got out for one reason—I did not like it! Similarly, nobody likes the cave of bitterness brought on by offense. The welcome light of God's wisdom is placed into your hands when you allow Him into your cave. But you have to let Him in! When you do, He will teach you three things when it seems the bats in the cave are about to swarm.

1. How to think like Jesus.
   "But we are those who have the mind of Christ" (1 Corinthians 2:16, JB).
2. How to act like Jesus.
   "Christ, who suffered for you, is your example. Follow in his steps: He never sinned, never told a lie, never answered back when insulted; when he suffered he did not threaten to get even; he left his case in the hands of God who always judges fairly" (1 Peter 2:21–23, TLB).

3. How to love like Jesus.

"Jesus knew that the time had come for him to leave this world and go to the Father. Having loved his own who were in the world, he now showed them the full extent of his love" (John 13:1, NIV).

The strength of your Christianity meets the ultimate test when you are offended. When you allow God into your pain, offenses will accelerate your spiritual growth because they force you into Christ-likeness at warp speed. You will emerge from your cave experience thinking, acting and loving more like Him. God will cause offenses to play a part in releasing your God-given destiny!

The Bigger Picture

I love to snorkel and have had the opportunity to do so in the beautiful, tropical waters of Hawaii. Before I placed the mask on my face and the breathing tube in my mouth, all I could see was blue water and waves stretching far into the horizon. If that was all I saw, I would not have been nearly as amazed. But the instant I put my head underneath the surface, a breathtaking, incredible view appeared. Thousands of multi-colored fish swam in teeming, swirling schools. Miles of gorgeous coral reef graced the underwater landscape. It was so beautiful that I never wanted to come up again!

Before I went beneath the surface, I could see only a fraction of what was there. But when I dove under I saw the *bigger picture*. Likewise, when a painful offense comes your way, remember Hawaiian waters. Far more lies beneath the surface of your situation than you can see. Beautiful, living truths are all around you—just beyond the natural eye.

God is going to make the pain of offense work for your good. He is going to teach you how to become like Jesus—and that is the most beautiful lesson of all. Always measure your hurts against the bigger picture. Say to yourself, "My life is bigger than this, my future is brighter. There is more here than meets the eye." Remember, more lies beneath the surface than you can see. God is at work in your pain.

> Remember, more lies beneath the surface than you can see. God is at work in your pain.

Paul knew God was using the mystery of suffering to perfect His work in him. This knowledge empowered him to remain ever focused on the bigger picture and rise above his circumstances. "Therefore most gladly I will rather boast in my infirmities, that the power of Christ may rest upon me" (2 Corinthians 12:9). You can do the same! You never will regret trusting God to send His light of wisdom into your suffering.

Suffering at the hands of men, battling in spiritual warfare and living in a sin-infected, demon-infested world are the realities through which we all navigate on a daily basis. The good news is that God uses our pain for His glory. He does not waste one tear or turn a deaf ear to our cries. "So that no man may be disturbed by these afflictions; for you yourselves know that we have been destined for this" (1 Thessalonians 3:3, NASB).

Chuck Swindoll observed, "God, in His sovereign and inscrutable plan, realized that pain had to be a part of our training program, so He destined it for us." A. W.

Tozer noted, "It is doubtful whether God can bless a man greatly until He has hurt him deeply."

Someone in Need Waits on the Other Side of Your Pain

One of the purposes God works through our pain is to give us a ministry to others who are hurting as we did. "What a wonderful God we have . . . the one who so wonderfully comforts and strengthens us in our hardships and trials" (2 Corinthians 1:3, TLB).

I praise God for comforting me in times of trouble, yet I also have learned that He has another purpose for making me whole. Paul continues: "And why does He do this? So that when others are troubled, needing our sympathy and encouragement, we can pass on to them this same help and comfort God has given us" (verse 4). When God blesses, comforts, helps or heals you, He also has others in mind. It is never just for you, nor only about you. God brings each of us through troubles and difficulties not only for our individual sakes, but also for the sakes of others whose paths we will cross.

> God brings each of us through troubles and difficulties not only for our individual sakes, but also for the sakes of others whose paths we will cross.

Hidden treasure lies in your pain! Those who have been hurt can help the hurting better than anyone else. I try to keep this in mind when I experience pain, because I have found that someone in need is always waiting on the other side of my recovery. The comfort I receive is a special gift-in-waiting for someone else.

151

God is going to bring you over to the other side of your offense. When you get there, you will be equipped to help others who are groping through the cave of offense. *Know* that.

But God sends another exciting flashlight into the cave of suffering—the light of His amazing grace! Let's look at it.

Follow-up Questions

1. In your "cave" experience, are you experiencing the light of God's knowledge? If so, what have you learned that you did not know before?
2. Do you *know* God is working through your suffering for your good and His glory? If you are unsure, why are you unsure? If you are sure, what do you see Him working so far?
3. Do you already see doors opening to help others since you began to be restored?

I encourage you to read Romans 8:28 slowly and thoughtfully. Let the power of its truth sink in.

16

The Light of Grace

I was once at a restaurant with some friends when we realized that our waiter either did not know what he was doing or did not care. He got almost all of our orders wrong, bringing me the wrong fish, one friend the wrong salad and the third a wrong side dish. When I asked him for some extra water, he never came back. I finally found a pitcher and poured my own. Even though my friends and I were low maintenance customers, the situation really got ridiculous.

After we chatted awhile, our wayward waiter sauntered up nonchalantly and handed us the check. We looked at one another and knew what we were all thinking—*the tip*. We had not been served well. Indeed, we had hardly been served at all. As waiters and service go, he had not earned a tip.

But a little voice deep down inside of me quietly speaks in times like this. It says, "Remember." And I

> But a little voice deep down inside of me quietly speaks in times like this. It says, "Remember."

do. I remember when I was a mess, did not know what I was going to do with my life and did not care. I remember, sometimes painfully, how I offended people, disappointed them and sometimes neglected them. And I vividly remember that God loved me when I did not love Him back. He kept working with me, forgave me, healed and restored me and gave me a future loaded with promise.

Having remembered, I left a decent tip and walked out. Who knows, maybe he had a day so bad that he could not concentrate or had heard some news that badly shook him. Service-wise the waiter did not have it coming, but that is when grace always steps in. Grace shows up when you do not deserve it.

What Has Grace Got to Do with It?

What does grace have to do with offenses? A lot! You are not going to get through the dark cave of offense without the guiding light of grace.

Let me explain. *Grace* literally means "undeserved favor." This is the word Paul used over and over again when explaining salvation. In our lost state, we could not hold a candle to that negligent waiter. Our sins toward God were light years beyond his shortcomings. "But God showed his great love for us by sending Christ to die for us while we were still sinners" (Romans 5:8, TLB).

God chose to save us, even while we were shaking our fists in His face. That is why His grace so aptly has been called *amazing*. It is totally undeserved, unearned and unmerited. It came because He decided to send it, period. Max Lucado, in his book *In the Grip Of Grace,* pointed out a few of the many blessings grace brings into our lives:

"You are beyond condemnation (see Romans 8:1).

You are delivered from the law (see Romans 7:6).

You are near God (see Ephesians 2:13).

You are delivered from the power of evil (see Colossians 1:13).

You are a member of his Kingdom (see Colossians 1:13).

You are justified (see Romans 5:1).

You are perfect (see Hebrews 10:14).

You have been adopted (see Romans 8:15).

You have access to God at any moment (see Ephesians 2:18).

You are a part of his priesthood (see 1 Peter 2:5).

You will never be abandoned (see Hebrews 13:5).

You have an imperishable inheritance (see 1 Peter 1:4).

You are a partner with Christ in life (see Colossians 3:4), privilege (see Ephesians 2:6), suffering (see 2 Timothy 2:12) and service (see 1 Corinthians 1:9).

You possess (Get this!) every imaginable spiritual blessing. 'In Christ, God has given us every spiritual blessing in the heavenly world' (Ephesians 1:3)."

The Giver and the Receiver

There are two sides to grace. The first involves the *giver* or *bestower* of grace. Someone must decide to give it before anyone can receive it. So since grace is undeserved favor, it can proceed only from a gracious, kind, merciful, loving and good heart. That is what the Bible says about God, and that is why it is called the "grace of God" in passage after passage. We are told that His is a "throne of grace" (Hebrews 4:16); that He gives "abundance of grace" (Romans 5:17); that His "grace is sufficient" for all trials (2 Corinthians 12:9); that His grace is rich (see Ephesians 1:7); that "good hope" springs from His grace (2 Thessalonians 2:16); that we are "saved" by grace (Ephesians 2:8); that we are "justified by His grace" (Titus 3:7); and that our hearts are "established by grace" (Hebrews 13:9). Grace, grace and more grace ever proceeds from the God of all grace, which tells us a whole lot about Him.

We are literally graced by grace!

The second aspect of grace involves the *receiver.* One meaning of the English word "grace" is "to decorate or dignify," and that is exactly what grace does for the recipient. Like a plain Christmas tree lovingly decorated with lights, bulbs and other beautiful, shiny, attractive ornaments, grace decorates our lives with all the above-mentioned blessings and much, much more. We are literally graced by grace!

But the amazing list does not stop with one-time, once-for-all gifts. Grace brings both immediate and long-term benefits. When we become God's children, His grace keeps working in us. We are literally under divine construction for the rest of our lives. We are ongoing works of grace. Always remember, *God is not finished with you yet.*

The Two-Pronged Blessing of Grace

Grace not only involves a giver and receiver, but it also delivers a two-pronged blessing. Paul explains this incredible good news in the following verse: "For God is at work within you, helping you want to obey him, and then helping you to do what he wants" (Philippians 2:13, TLB). Two ideas leap out at me from this verse—*desire* and *power*. God's grace brings both the desire and power to do God's will.

The Divine "Wanna Do"

Like the flashlight to which I held so tightly in the cave, grace is one of the lights God extends to us in our caves of offense. And that grace influences our *desires*. Even though the temptation can be overwhelming to respond to offense in all the wrong ways, the grace of God touches your heart, creating a longing to do the right thing. God's grace working on your heart is one powerful fact going for you in your suffering.

Grace changes your inward *"want to."* It influences your desires, turning your motivations toward Him. Grace steps in and changes all the old, carnal instincts. Once we belong to God, what we want in life, what drives us and the inner longings of our soul undergo a steady, grace-driven change. Over time, grace transforms it all. It is what I call the *"divine wanna do."* A grace-touched heart cries out with King David, "I delight to do your will, O my God!" (Psalm 40:8, AMPLIFIED).

I can remember an almost immediate change in the things I desired after I turned my life over to Christ. It was not that I was suddenly and completely delivered from all temptations or fleshly appetites. Like you, I still do and always will have struggles with the flesh. But a new set of desires began to grow in the seedbed of my soul. A burning to read God's Word, to spend time with Him in prayer and to live a life pleasing to Him steadily emerged. God uses heaven-sent desire to stir us out of our caves of pain and to motivate us to obey His will.

Jeremiah understood this side of grace well. After Israel had consistently rejected his words of warning about impending judgment, the prophet awoke one day ready to toss in the towel. He complained, "I am in derision daily; everyone mocks me" (Jeremiah 20:7).

> God uses heaven-sent desire to stir us out of our caves of pain and to motivate us to obey His will.

Jeremiah felt totally alone. I can almost hear him say, "You can take this prophet stuff and give it to someone who likes punishment. I've had it!" At the height of his frustration, he wanted to cry: "I will not make mention of Him, nor speak anymore in His name" (verse 9).

That sounds to me like a pretty good case of the quits! It makes me feel better, because I have been there myself. I am so thankful that God tells us the truth about His servants. He does not candy coat their humanity or leave out the dirty stuff. We are allowed to see His people in all their imperfections. Jeremiah's cry of frustration echoed from the pit of his cave experience. But listen closely to Jeremiah's own testimony of the divine "wanna do" working on his heart. "But His word was in my heart like a burning fire shut up in my bones; I was weary of holding it back, and I could not" (verse 9).

Though his offended emotions raged, something stronger entered the corridors of his cave of suffering and moved Jeremiah out—*a holy passion to declare God's Word*. That God-sent "heartburn," the heavenly passion to serve God, overcame all the fiery attacks of the enemy. It was the *divine wanna do* within Jeremiah that made all the difference. My point is this: The same light of motivating grace is shining in you right now, touching your heart to handle offense His way, moving you out of your cave into the sunshine of freedom. If it were not so, you probably would not be reading this book! Like a king holding a scepter of favor toward you, His amazing grace is extended right now to aid you through your painful offense.

The Divine "Can Do"

If you have ever been in a gym where people are working out with weights, you probably know the function of a spotter. A spotter is someone who stands behind you just before you lift a lot of weight. He is there in case the weight becomes too much for you. When you start to cave, the spotter steps in, grabs the bar and helps you lift it up again. He helps you to lift what you cannot lift on your own, saving you from being crushed by the weight you are under.

The Holy Spirit is God's spotter. Remember that Christmas tree I mentioned, decorated with many different ornaments? One of the great gifts with which the grace of God "decorates" you is the Holy Spirit living within, and one of the Holy Spirit's many functions is to strengthen you. God's Spirit, there by undeserved favor, steps in and empowers you to lift the weights of life you cannot lift on your own—like the crushing weight of a painful offense. "For if you live according to the flesh you will die; but if by the Spirit you put to death the deeds of the body, you will live" (Romans 8:13).

Grace creates the desire to please God, and grace empowers you to live it out by the ministry of the Holy Spirit. Adversity that would normally take you down is conquered through the divine spotter of the Holy Spirit. He says, "C'mon, push! I am here to help you. You can do it!" Out of nowhere, you discover the ability to lift what you thought was impossible. A sudden surge of strength emerges in the midst of pain and confusion, and you find yourself lifting, lifting and lifting again until you are not only free, but you are also stronger than ever before!

> Grace creates the desire to please God, and grace empowers you to live it out by the ministry of the Holy Spirit.

God will not give you a desire without empowering you to carry it through to fulfillment. Through the mighty Holy Spirit, grace empowers you to live out God-sent desires. Helping you *want to*, and then helping you *to do*—that is grace! Grace produces in us both the *desire* to do God's will, and the *divine empowering* to rise above every obstacle.

When you receive the flashlight of God's grace, you discover the strength to rise above your weaknesses and forgive your offenders, even to the place of praying for them! By repeated personal experience, Paul proclaimed: "For I can do everything God asks me to do with the help of Christ who gives me the strength and power" (Philippians. 4:13, TLB). Grace is there when the rubber of your weakness meets the road of God's requirements to forgive.

In the pain and confusion of shattered relationships, grace grabs on and places within us both the *divine wanna do* and the *ability to do* His will. When you have been offended, you can count on the spotter to be there.

> Grace is there when the rubber of your weakness meets the road of God's requirements to forgive.

Yes, you will still feel the pain. Yes, you will struggle with anger and other "bats" in the cave of offense. Yet His grace is there in the darkness of the cave, illuminating the dangers and strengthening you to avoid the trap of bitterness.

But that is not all of the benefits that can come out of your painful experience with offense. We have looked at the flashlights of wisdom and grace; now let's consider another light that is truly exciting!

Follow-up Questions

1. In what ways are you experiencing God's grace in your cave of suffering?
2. Are you aware of the "Divine Wanna Do" working in you? If so, what desire is God using to help pull you out?
3. Have you sensed God's power to enable you to do the right thing? How have you responded to it?

I encourage you to embrace His grace by responding in faith to what He is doing in your heart.

---17---

The Light of Transformation

Amy sat across from me with tears flowing freely. Dabbing her eyes with a handkerchief, she told me one of the most difficult stories I have ever heard. About a year before her visit to my office, she had waved goodbye to her husband, John, and her two stepchildren, 32-year-old Sue and 22-year-old Bob. John had been in ministry for many years but also did other things to put bread on the table. Though they had their struggles, Amy and John were happy and moving forward in life.

A few days before Christmas, John had been scheduled to deliver furniture to a client in Corpus Christi, Texas, as one of his part-time jobs. He asked Bob to go along and also felt compelled to ask his daughter, Sue, to go with them. Sue had been having some problems with depression, and John was concerned.

The night they arrived in Corpus Christi, John called Amy to touch base and say goodnight, as was his habit. No one knows exactly what happened in the small hotel room afterward, only that the following morning the housekeeper knocked several times with no response and finally opened the door. Upon entering, her eyes fell on a scene she would never forget. John and Bob were lying dead, both shot in the head. The police arrived to find Sue on the bathroom floor, also dead from what was ruled a self-inflicted gunshot wound. There were no signs of a struggle or of forced entry. For some inexplicable reason, Sue had killed her father and brother and then turned the gun on herself.

As Amy told me of her heartbreaking ordeal, I could not imagine what she had gone through—the call from the police, the initial shock and disbelief, the accompanying flood of questions as to how such a thing could have happened—all must have been unbearable. The knowledge that she would never speak with her three loved ones again combined with the anger and heartbreak over Sue's unthinkable actions were gigantic hurdles for this quiet Christian woman to overcome.

Amy slowly grabbed another Kleenex from the top of my desk. Leaning back and wiping away the tears, she told me about the dreaded visit to the funeral home. Walking numbly into the viewing room, she looked at the bodies of John, Bob and Sue. It was surreal, like a scene from a bad movie. Then she said something that I will always remember as a tremendous testimony to God's grace. Walking over to Sue's coffin, she peered in at the lifeless figure and knew what she must do.

"Sue, I forgive you. I don't know how you could have done it, and I'll probably never understand what possessed you, but I forgive you," she choked out.

Sue had taken three lives, but Amy was not going to allow her to take a fourth by exiling her to the cave of bitterness. She went on to describe how the anger instantly dissipated, and she was freed from the groping tentacles of bitterness. Amy has been through much counseling and inner healing since then, but one thing with which she has never had to deal is the poisonous serpent of bitterness. Through a tragedy, God transformed her by making her more Christ-like than ever. Her story reminded me of a truth I have seen repeated over and over: God sends the shining promise of positive transformation into the cave of painful offense.

The Promise of Transformation

An ancient king placed a boulder on a roadway and then hid himself and watched to see if anyone would remove the huge rock. Some of the king's wealthiest merchants and courtiers came and simply walked around it. Many loudly blamed the king for not keeping the roads clear. But none did anything about getting the stone out of the way.

Finally a peasant came along carrying a load of vegetables. Upon approaching the boulder, the peasant laid down his burden and tried to move the stone to the side of the road. After much pushing and straining, he finally succeeded. When the peasant picked up his load again, he noticed a purse in the road where the boulder had been. It contained many gold coins and a note from the king indicating that the reward was for the person who had removed the boulder from the roadway. The peasant learned a valuable lesson that many of us overlook: Every obstacle in your path presents an opportunity to improve your condition.

When we discussed the light of wisdom in chapter 15 we touched on the promise of transforming change. This is a third light in the cave. Your offense is not going to break you; it is going to make you. God's intent is to change you, and He will use everything at His disposal to do it—even offenses.

> Every obstacle in your path presents an opportunity to improve your condition.

Let's take our eyes off of your offender for a moment, okay? Just for a moment let's pretend he or she does not exist. Right now—and always—God's focus is you, your response to life's issues and what He is developing in you through the offenses you experience. God wants to change you. As with Amy, even devastating events can become powerful opportunities for God's greater work. This powerful promise shines through every dark storm cloud of life.

I am not saying God causes bad things to happen. What I am saying is that He uses the good, the bad and the ugly to bring about a greater result in those who put their trust in Him. If you trust God in the midst of your trial, He will use it to transform you into the image of His Son!

I have learned something through the years: If I cannot change painful circumstances, God will use them to change me. I may not be able to change the person who hurt me, but I can change. I cannot control the actions of people, but I can control my response to them. In all honesty, I do not always like that. I have battled against offense like anyone else. When someone has hurt me, I wanted to see him or her change. And, in all honesty, at times I have wanted to see the person "get his." After all, why should I have to be the spiritual one? Inner change, even with the help of God's grace, is not always easy. Yet the fact is that God is in the transforming business, and changing us is the way He most often delivers us.

> God is in the transforming business, and changing us is the way He most often delivers us.

I know what you are thinking. "But Jeff, God delivers His people *out of* difficulties. He is a delivering God!" I agree—God can and does deliver us out of some of our circumstances. But more times than not His way of choice is to change *us* before changing our circumstances. Circumstances may or may not ever change, but *we* can always change.

Scan the Scriptures and look at the major players. From Abraham to Moses, to David and the prophets, down through the New Testament apostles—all found themselves in difficult circumstances that God did not at first change. He chose instead to transform them. Once they changed, He often changed their circumstances. But then again, sometimes He did not. Did Paul's "thorn" ever leave (see 2 Corinthians 12:8, 9)? There is no indication of that. What about the second half of Hebrews 11? Read it lately? We do not hear much about it, but it is just as important as the first half because it gives the balance of truth on this important issue. Saints with just as much faith as those mentioned in the first half were tortured, mocked, scourged, chained and imprisoned, stoned, cut in half, killed by the sword and called mountains and caves their home (see Hebrews 11:35–38). Why were they not delivered from their circumstances? I cannot answer that, but I do know this—they were transformed! Nothing can touch us that God will not use to bring dynamic transformation—this is the beauty and power of Christianity!

Do you know why this is true? God decreed this would be the case before the worlds were formed! My mind cannot wrap around the following verses, but listen to what the Bible teaches about God's plan for us. Before Jehovah God flung countless stars into space, scooped out the vast, blue oceans or skillfully chiseled out the awesome mountain ranges, *He saw you redeemed in Christ.* "Just as He chose us in Him before the foundation of the world, that we should be holy and without blame before Him" (Ephesians 1:4).

And there is more! Before time began, when everything you see, hear, taste, touch and smell were only ideas in His unfathomable mind, *God decreed that you would be conformed into the image of His Son.* "For whom He foreknew, He also predestined to be conformed to the image of His Son" (Romans 8:29).

> Always remember: God's never-ending quest is to transform us into the image of His Son.

Hold on for more. God's decree was so firm, so rock solid that He declared *all things* would serve that purpose. As mentioned in chapter 15, this includes not only the good things, but also the things that threaten, anger, perplex and pain you. All must bow to His ultimate will! "And we know that all things work together for good to those who love God, to those who are the called according to His purpose" (Romans 8:28).

Always remember: God's never-ending quest is to transform us into the image of His Son. Every circumstance is a hammer and chisel in His mighty hands. Every situation is a part of the paintbrush by which He colors the canvas of our lives. Each experience, no matter how small or great, is the knitting needle that God uses to crochet a masterpiece of balance and beauty. And He does all of this without taking away our individuality. Making us more like Christ actually enhances our uniqueness. Though we are not always delivered "out of" difficulties, inward change is often the trigger that releases God to change our circumstances. Think about it:

- God did not deliver Moses *from* the backside of the desert. He changed him *in* the desert, and then brought him *out* of it to deliver a nation.
- God did not deliver David from the long days and lonely nights of running from King Saul on the Judean hillsides. He changed *him* first—maturing, strengthening and seasoning him within the crucible of his circumstances—then He changed his circumstances, placing the kingly crown on his head.
- Shadrach, Meshach and Abednego were not delivered *from* the fiery oven. God delivered them *in the fire* first (when the fourth man appeared), then delivered them *from it*. But their greatest victory came *in* the oven.
- Paul was not immediately delivered out of jail. Yet while still in those stench-filled, wretched dungeons, he wrote the triumphant epistles, telling millions through the ages to "rejoice always"

The Light of Transformation

and "in everything give thanks" (1 Thessalonians 5:16, 18).

God very well may deliver us "out of." But until He does, He wants to transform us! "Do not conform any longer to the pattern of this world, but be transformed by the renewing of your mind" (Romans 12:2, NIV).

I do not know your current situation, what hurt you or how long it has gone on. But I do know this—a light is being extended to you. Not only the lights of wisdom and grace, but also a shining promise—God is going to transform you!

Three Survival Keys

Let me offer three simple keys to experiencing transformation in your trials. Your response to God is crucial to the transformation He wants to bring.

- Do not become bitter toward Him.
- Do not allow your pain to cause you to drift from Him.
- Praise Him in the midst of it all.

I am not being flippant or formulaic when I suggest these three survival keys. Pain has a funny way of working against us unless we make up our minds how we will respond to it. Remember Part 3? *Response is everything!* In fact, I am reminded of a man who had every reason to be bitter but responded beautifully to terrible mistreatment at the hands of his own brothers. He models the last light that God sends into our cave of suffering—the light of inner healing.

Follow-up Questions

1. What do you suspect God wants to change in you in your current ordeal?
2. Have you been tempted to conform to the world in the way you responded to your offense? If so, how can you turn it around?
3. Do you see the value in responding in a way that brings transformation? Explain.

I encourage you to read Romans 12:1–3 slowly, allowing its powerful truths to spur you on toward transformation.

18

The Light of Inner Healing

God is a Healer. He not only heals sick, afflicted bodies, but He heals the hidden, festering wounds of the heart—those aches that run deep as a result of hurts brought on through the fallout of relationships gone sour. God heals the biting, lingering pain left by offenses.

> God heals the biting, lingering pain left by offenses.

As the prophet Isaiah peered down the tunnel of time to the day the Messiah would come to earth, he predicted several characteristics of His ministry. He would preach, heal, deliver, comfort and plant (see Isaiah 61:1–3). But listen to the prediction of Christ's healing ministry. "The Spirit of the Lord GOD is upon Me . . . He has sent Me to heal the brokenhearted" (verse 1).

"Heal" is taken from a Hebrew word meaning "to bind up." The idea is to "wrap around" something as one would wrap a turban or a medicinal wrapping such as a medicated compress. For instance, we all have seen, either in person or perhaps in a movie or television show, a wounded limb wrapped around by a wet compress that brought relief to the suffering. Isaiah prophesied that Christ would wrap broken hearts with His healing touch, binding them up into wholeness once again. In essence, he foresaw that one of Christ's major ministries would be the healing of painful memories. But this predicted ministry of the Messiah was not exclusive to the New Testament. Many in the Old Testament experienced the healing of wounded memories as well.

Joseph, the Model of Response

You might remember the story of the patriarch Joseph—how his eleven cold-hearted brothers betrayed him, selling him into Egyptian slavery (see Genesis 37–50). As one sin usually leads to another, they then lied to his brokenhearted father, Jacob, telling him that wild animals had killed his beloved son.

The list of offenses perpetrated on Joseph is lengthy. Here are just a few. He was:

- cast into a deep pit by his brothers who intended to let him die there.
- sold up the river into Egyptian slavery by the same brothers.
- falsely accused of attempted rape by Potiphar's wife.
- thrown into prison for two full years on the bogus attempted rape charge, during which time "they

hurt his feet with fetters, he was laid in irons"
(Psalm 105:18).

- forgotten by Pharaoh's chief butler and baker, whose
dreams he interpreted during their stay in prison,
in spite of Joseph's heart-wrenching entreaties.

"Cast down," "sold out," "accused of," "thrown into"
and "forgotten" all are words describing the ill treat-
ment Joseph experienced at the hands of others. Yet his
testimony to God's healing of harsh, painful memories
is magnificent. After many years of trials and hardship,
God favored Joseph with an incredible promotion.
Pharaoh experienced two disturbing dreams and could
find no one to interpret them. Joseph was summoned
at the suggestion of the chief butler, who suddenly
remembered him, and interpreted their meaning.
Because of his supernatural gift, he was promoted
and became second only to Pharaoh in all the land
of Egypt.

Joseph's Legacy—Forgetful and Fruitful

In both the Old and New Testaments, the names
given to children were always filled with meaning. For
instance, *Moses* meant "drawn out" as a testimony that
he was rescued from the waters of the Nile River. It also
signified that he would be a rescuer, which came to pass
in spades when he took over one million people out of
Egyptian bondage. Another Bible character was named
Jabez, which meant "he will cause pain." Jabez was given
this unenviable name because his mother's labor was
apparently very difficult (see 1 Chronicles 4:10).

About thirteen years after his brothers first sold him away, Joseph had two sons. The names he gave them were hugely autobiographical. He named his first son *Manasseh*, meaning "making forgetful." Of him Joseph said, "For God has made me forget all my toil and all my father's house" (Genesis 41:51).

Forgetful, therefore, was the crowning testimony of a healed man. It shouts of the goodness and faithfulness of a God who removed the sting of painful memories caused by all the mistreatment Joseph had experienced. You know you have been healed of offense when the memory no longer stings.

> You know you have been healed of offense when the memory no longer stings.

Joseph was not saying that he literally did not remember his imprisonment or his father, Jacob. Healing of the memories does not entail some kind of divine amnesia. It simply means that no more pain is associated with the events that so crushed you at the start. You remember, but you no longer hurt from it. That sickening feeling of an aching, broken heart is gone. Your mind is able to put it all to rest without constantly rehashing the painful events. You are free! When Joseph remembered all the wrongs done to him, he experienced no anger, no sting, no hurt and no pain. This was so real to him that his first son's name was a living memorial to the miracle of healed memories.

Joseph named his second son *Ephraim*, meaning "fruitfulness." Of Ephraim he said, "For God has made me fruitful in the land of my affliction" (verse 52). God did not stop with the healing of painful memories. He made Joseph fruitful in the very land in which his brothers had hoped to destroy him. It brings to mind the well-known verse from the Twenty-third Psalm. "You prepare a table before me in the presence of my enemies" (Psalm 23:5). God does not just heal us; He makes us victorious in plain view of our befuddled enemies!

The very thing with which Satan tries to destroy us is what God most uses to reveal His power in us. Through the dark valleys of failure, betrayal, pain, disappointment and disillusionment, God brings us to the other side not only intact but "more than conquerors" (Romans 8:37). *Listen:* In the place of your greatest pain, God is going to bring your greatest victory. The place of bitter tears and dark valleys will become a testimony, a land of fruitfulness, a place of Satan's defeat and a mark of God's power. Can you think of anything more vexing to your enemy than for you to prosper in the place in which he planned to destroy you?

> Can you think of anything more vexing to your enemy than for you to prosper in the place in which he planned to destroy you?

The enemy plotted and schemed to destroy Joseph in Egypt, yet instead he became prime minister! I picture Joseph calling his children to himself at the end of a long day. "Come sit in Daddy's lap, Fruitful! Give me a big hug, Forgetful!" Each time he looked at them he was reminded of the goodness of the God who healed the pain of his past and prospered him in the land of his affliction.

Saved by Wisdom

The Bible records that after Jacob's death, Joseph's eleven brothers feared for their lives. With Dad gone,

Joseph might seek vengeance! Instead, Joseph responded with a profoundly insightful statement: "But as for you, you meant evil against me; but God meant it for good, in order to bring it about as it is this day, to save many people alive" (Genesis 50:20).

Catch that as you would catch a bag of gold thrown your way, because the same goes for you, too! Joseph had a secret that kept him free from the bite of bitterness: *He obtained wisdom from God in the midst of his trials.* God opened Joseph's understanding to recognize His mighty hand at work through all the offenses hurled at him. It was not the ways and means that Joseph would have chosen, but David the psalmist tells us who was behind the whole drama. "He [God] sent a man before them—Joseph—who was sold as a slave" (Psalm 105:17).

Betrayed by his brothers, sold as a slave, despised, forgotten and cast into jail for something he did not do, Joseph could have lived and died a bitter man.

Joseph's story is an incredible testimony of God's staggering sovereignty. He wanted Joseph in Egypt and used his brothers to get him there, turning their evil intentions for a divine purpose. They thought they were getting rid of him forever, but actually *God was sending Joseph to Egypt.* Bound with chains, carried away in the back of an Egyptian caravan as the cruel faces of his eleven brothers faded in the distance, Joseph probably did not see God's hand in it at the time. But the Almighty was weaving His incredible plan through it all.

Betrayed by his brothers, sold as a slave, despised, forgotten and cast into jail for something he did not do, Joseph could have lived and died a bitter man. But he did not. Joseph sought God in his pain, and the curtain separating the natural world from the spiritual was lifted, allowing him to peer into the mysterious workings of Providence. *God meant it for good.* The shining light of wisdom in the cave of offense lit his way! He came to understand that he was raised up to save the nation of Egypt from starvation. And, more importantly, he was God's chosen instrument to preserve the embryonic Hebrew race, represented by his father and eleven brothers—the race that later would usher in the Messiah!

Like Joseph, we need God's insight into our trials. This is why James exhorted, "If any of you lacks wisdom, let him ask of God, who gives to all liberally and without reproach, and it will be given to him" (James 1:5). Ask for wisdom about what? The trials in which you find yourself. God will lift the curtain to reveal what He is accomplishing *through* them. His wisdom will carry you out of the cave into the sunshine once again.

Burn the Urn

The prophet Isaiah also predicted that the coming Messiah would give "beauty for ashes" (Isaiah 61:3). Before his deliverance from prison and ultimate promotion, Joseph's life certainly looked like a pile of ashes. In the natural he would have been tagged a has-been. Yet God took the ashes of rejection, betrayal and heartbreak and brought beauty out of it all. But He did something else that we, too, must do in order to experience the same miracle: In order to receive the beauty God has for us, we have got to give Him the ashes!

In our culture when someone is cremated, the deceased's loved ones often place his or her ashes in an urn that they then place in a visible spot to keep the person's memory alive. But this is just what you do not want to do with the ashes left in the wake of a painful offense. Never place the ashes from pain and hurt into an urn, memorializing the offense!

Many have never received beauty for ashes because they coddle the events that hurt them, never truly giving them to Jesus. It often becomes a martyr's syndrome. We wear our hurt on our sleeves and fall into the trap of seeking sympathy from people everywhere we go, actually becoming known for our pain.

I do not want to give offenses that kind of power, do you? I would rather be known as a positive person who has moved beyond the pains of my past. To do that, we must "burn the urn." Get rid of it! We must not hold onto anything that memorializes an offense as if it were sacred. It is a divine exchange; we give Him the ashes, and He will do something new and wonderful.

> Eventually we will sense the mighty hand of the One who gives beauty for ashes, lifting the pain and infection from our hearts.

How often must we give Him the ashes? As often as is necessary. Some days we may have to give Him the pain and devastation a hundred times. We must do it anyway! Eventually we will sense the mighty hand of the One who gives beauty for ashes, lifting the pain and infection from our hearts.

Peace will replace the churning, painful emotions, followed by the glorious realization that the sting is gone. Ultimately we will prosper in the land of our pain!

Do you feel as if you are in a dark cave of offense? Are the dogs of biting emotions and growling memories nipping at your heels, threatening your peace of mind, your relationships or your walk with God? *Do not give up—there is hope!* Remember the lights that God sends: *wisdom, grace, transformation* and *inner healing.* You will come out of the cave of suffering. The devastation of offense eventually will evaporate before the light of obedience to His word.

But, oh, I almost forgot. I never told you the rest of my story concerning that little theft thing. Okay, let's briefly look at whether you will be a David or a Saul, and I will finish my tale.

Follow-up Questions

1. As you have read this book, have you become aware of inner healing taking place as it did with Joseph? If so, how?
2. How far have you gone in seeking God's wisdom about your trial of offense?
3. Has He spoken? If so, what benefits has He shown you?

I encourage you to seek Him with all your heart for the wisdom you need to see your trial of offense through His eyes.

Will You Be a David or a Saul?

Do not, I beg you, only hear the message, but put it into practice.

James 1:22, PME

Sooner or later, we all will decide whether to be a Saul or a David when faced with offense. What is the difference? Well, you probably remember the story. One day, after King Saul had brought the young giant killer, David, into his kingdom and army, he heard the women of Israel singing a song that shot to the top of the Israeli hit list and changed his life forever. The stanza went like this: "Saul has slain his thousands, and David his ten thousands" (1 Samuel 18:7).

They were dancing in the streets while they sang, which did not give Saul a warm, fuzzy feeling. The Bible says, "Saul eyed David from that day forward" (verse 9). The green-eyed monster of red-hot jealousy raised his ugly head, and Saul became deeply offended. Things quickly went from bad to worse. After first trying to kill David by hurling javelins at him, Saul became the first Old Testament stalker, hounding David for ten long years in the lonely wilderness of Judea.

When you study the two men, very different individuals emerge in terms of their response to offense. Saul retaliated; David did not. Saul lashed out in vengeance; David trusted God. Saul hurled spears to hurt others; David drove out demons and brought peace. Saul was insecure in his position; David trusted his lot to God. Saul was made worse by offenses; David grew in maturity.

Saul's offense ultimately drove him down the dark corridors of madness. The end of his life is a tragedy, as we find him consulting a medium for counsel instead of turning to the living God (see 1 Samuel 28:8–25). He died a tragic death at the hands of the Philistines, taking his son and David's best friend, Jonathan, with him. Yet David only grew stronger. He refused to curse Saul or to take vengeance into his own hands (see 1 Samuel 24:6). He only blessed Saul during heart-wrenching, brief encounters. After turning his enemy over to God and patiently enduring ten long years of exile in the Judean wilderness, David became king of Israel.

One of life's great tests is how you choose to handle your enemies.

One of life's great tests is how you choose to handle your enemies. You can *react* like Saul or *respond* like

David. The answer will determine a great deal about your future. Enemies will come and offenses will happen to all of us. But will you be a Saul or a David? How will you respond?

Do you recall the Teflon response discussed in chapter 12? Jesus said, "But I say to you, *love* your enemies, *bless* those who curse you, *do good* to those who hate you, and *pray* for those who spitefully use you and persecute you" (Matthew 5:44). Love, bless, do good to and pray for your offenders. These responses to being wronged, like the Teflon pan, keep the offense from sticking, especially when practiced immediately. The apostle Paul faced more offenses than most and added a few addendums to the Teflon response worth noting before we close.

Addendum #1: Leave Vengeance to God

"Repay no one evil for evil. . . . Beloved, do not avenge yourselves, but rather give place to wrath; for it is written, 'Vengeance is Mine, I will repay,' says the Lord'" (Romans 12:17, 19). As believers we are commanded to resist falling into the trap of retaliation—not openly, not subtly, not secretly, *not at all.* God claims all rights to the vengeance market! This is not "Wimp Class 101" either. Rather, it is understanding a timeless principle: If we retaliate, God takes His hands off the situation, and we are on our own.

> If we retaliate, God takes His hands off the situation, and we are on our own.

It is not that He ceases to care—He always does. But when we step across the line by taking vengeance into our own hands we get into trouble, just as I did with those ravenous dogs. We transgress against that little four-word command tucked away in the verse above: "Give place to wrath." The Phillips Modern English version says, "Stand back and let God punish if he will." The Jerusalem Bible says, "Never try to get revenge; leave that, my friends, to God's anger."

Annie Chapman in her book *A Woman's Answer to Anger* aptly observes:

> Human forgiveness, on the other hand, is simply forfeiting the right to revenge. The release is experienced only for the one who forgives. When we forgive, we are disconnecting ourselves from the offender. We are the one who is set free.

As David discovered, God deals with our enemies if we stay out of the way. Leaving your situation in God's hands is the only way to keep your heart free. The outcome is up to Him. Remember, God sees wrongdoing, abuse and unfairness. And He sees the wrongs done in His Church. He is watching your situation—He really is!

This is not to say that you should tolerate physical or emotional abuse. There is a great difference between protecting yourself from cruel, evil abuse and taking vengeance into your own hands. David rightly hid himself from Saul in the wilderness caves of En Gedi by the Dead Sea. He did not allow Saul to harm or kill him. At the same time, however, he refused to take vengeance. There is a delicate balance between the two, and God will show you the difference. Sometimes you can and should protect yourself from abuse.

You probably have wondered what happened to the man who stole our money and how I have handled the offense since then. A few months after the ten thousand dollars were stolen and my stunning encounter with the perpetrator on the phone, the news came to me that he had filed bankruptcy and lost his business. Bankruptcy, as you probably know, is a seven-year ordeal. Your financial life dries up, while you face the daunting task of totally rebuilding your credit. I did not rejoice in what I heard, however, and I will tell you why.

Addendum #2: Do Not Rejoice When God Brings Judgment

"Do not rejoice when your enemy falls, and do not let your heart be glad when he stumbles; lest the LORD see it, and it displease Him, and He turn away His wrath from him" (Proverbs 24:17–18). Paul chimed in by quoting a related proverb: "If your enemy is hungry, feed him; if he thirsts, give him a drink; for in so doing you will heap coals of fire on his head" (Romans 12:20). God not only commands us to turn our enemies over to Him, but He also expects us to maintain a right attitude when He judges them.

> God not only commands us to turn our enemies over to Him, but He also expects us to maintain a right attitude when He judges them.

Think about it. What a waste to respond successfully to our offenders by practicing the Teflon response, only to see God turn His judgment away because of a wrong attitude on our part! If we rejoice in their pain instead of sorrowing that their sin has brought them to such a place, God pulls back. Such an attitude brings the whole process to a halt. All our efforts to handle an offense scripturally are thwarted!

185

As mentioned in chapter 1, it was a tremendous battle for me to give this man to the Lord in daily prayer. I did not ask for judgment but simply turned him over to God, releasing my anger and hurt to Him. But it was not easy. Our phone conversation would jump into my head at the most unexpected moments, and all the emotions came with it. His cavalier attitude and lack of remorse and repentance, as well as the apparent lack of concern from his pastor, replayed over and over in the theater of my mind. The only way to turn off the recorder was the Teflon response. *Love, bless, do good to and pray for your offender.*

Eventually, like Joseph, the sting was gone when I thought of it, and God did indeed bless me in the place of my affliction! But did the dogs come after me? Yes! Did I go into the cave? Almost! Did I need the lights of wisdom, grace, transformation and inner healing to get me through it? Oh, yes!

Addendum #3: Yield to the Jesus within You

I admit that the temptation to rejoice rose within me upon hearing what happened to him. I remembered God's Word, however, and leaned on Him. In fact, I learned that one of the great keys to a victorious attitude is to yield to the Christ living within you! Jesus can love *through you.* He can forgive the offenders in your life. He can bless those who hurt you. I prayed, "Lord, help him. He really needs it. And help me. I am really struggling with it!" More than once I defeated the temptation to tell his story with any delight, or to rejoice over his loss by just yielding to Jesus.

When offense knocks, you can either send Adam— your old flesh—to the door, or you can send Jesus. If Jesus answers, the offense will quietly leave and the door will shut. If Adam answers, the offense will come in with all its baggage and take up residence in your house. This is why Paul admonished, "Do not be overcome by evil, but overcome evil with good" (Romans 12:21).

Admittedly, I have never understood how he has not returned to repent, or why his pastor never contacted me with any kind of encouragement or closure. But our church went on growing, and my heart stayed free. God has been good. We have never been late on a bill and have always had enough. In fact, as of this writing we have paid off our building and are gloriously debt-free. When I think of how retaliation could have consumed my time and sidetracked me from God's will, I am thankful I left the vengeance market to Him!

Remember, do not retaliate, and do not rejoice when your enemy falls. When you are wronged, practice yielding to the Jesus within you. God is much bigger and stronger than your raging emotions and will reward you for doing things His way. Do not be a vengeful, angry Saul. Make the choice to be a gracious, trusting David!

A Final Snapshot

My son, Jeremy, played T-ball as a child. T-ball is baseball for kids as young as five years old. Instead of pitching, the ball is placed in a little holder in front of the batter. The fledgling player eyes it carefully, swings, hopes to connect and then runs the bases like normal baseball. It is a kick! As a dad, I have some wonderful memories of Jeremy's T-ball games.

One day a lasting memory was made. Jeremy's team had one point on their competitor. It was the last inning, bases were loaded, there were two outs, and the other guys were up to bat. Their last hitter hauled off and swatted the ball way out into left field—the best hit of the game. Every eye watched it sail toward a little fella whose hat seemed to swallow his whole head. I did not recognize him, but T-ball in our neck of the woods did not have rigid rules—you could join at any time in the season. The "hat" saw it coming, ran toward it and just barely missed the game-winning catch. It plopped down just in front of him, rolling right into his glove. One runner had crossed the plate already, but there was still time to throw home and tie the game. Everyone in the stands was yelling, "Throw it! Throw it!"

To the astonishment of all, the little guy pulled it close, hunkered down and held on to it like a prize diamond! He seemed to be saying, "I've waited all afternoon for this thing, and I'm not about to let go of it now!" The crowd went nuts. "Throw it! Hurry up!" All to no avail. I thought our coach was going to have a coronary on the spot. The entire game was reduced to this final play. As the stunned crowd watched, the remaining runners crossed home plate one by one, giving them the win. An entire bleacher of angry eyes was fixed on the little guy in left field still holding the ball.

About this time a tall, stately man came out of the stands and walked slowly toward him. *Dad.* His father stooped down and hugged him as he stubbornly clutched the ball. Then his dad began speaking while moving his hands at the same time. *Sign language.* A hush fell over the stands.

"It's okay, son, give me the ball," I heard him say, moving his hands at the same time.

Embarrassed heads bowed. The little boy looked his dad in the face, tears streaming, and slowly turned over the coveted ball. I gulped as reality hit me in the gut. He simply did not get it. He did not understand the game. In his child's mind, he just wanted the ball. And he did not hear the crowd. He could not. He was deaf.

You Have to Understand the Game

Like that little boy, many Christians hold on to offenses because they do not understand the game. They just do not get that we are to throw offenses "home" to Jesus. Instead of hanging onto it, we are to cast it onto Him. This is the way the game of life is played.

And like that boy, we do not hear the Scriptures shouting from the grandstands, "Release the offense! Throw it home!" The offense has deafened us to the voice of God, dulling our spiritual senses.

But here is the good news. Eventually our heavenly Father walks out to us on the playing field of life, kneels down and says, "It's okay, child. You can give me the ball." Is He saying that to you? Has He spoken to your heart through this book? Is His Spirit dealing with you about an offense? Isn't it time to put an end to it?

If the answer is yes, then I encourage you to give the offense to Jesus. It can all turn in your favor right now. Go ahead—give Him the ball!

189

Follow-up Questions

1. Why should you be a David instead of a Saul? What are the short- and long-term benefits?
2. How do you know you have given your offense to Jesus instead of hanging onto it?
3. In what ways has this book changed your thinking about offenses?

I encourage you to be a doer of what you have read and allow Christ to transform you and bring inner healing to your soul!

Bibliography

Barna, George. *The Second Coming of the Church*. Nashville: Word Publishing, 1998.

Bevere, John. *The Bait of Satan*. Lake Mary, Fla.: Creation House, 1994.

Chapman, Annie. *A Woman's Answer to Anger*. Eugene, Ore.: Harvest House Publishers, 2000.

Collins, Gary R. "When Anger Turns To Bitterness," from the American Association of Christian Counselors website: <www.aacc.net>.

Hornsby, Bill. "Casualties in the Church." Bethany Cell Church Network newsletter, February 17, 2000.

Johnson, Barbara. *Stick a Geranium in Your Hat and Be Happy*. Dallas: Word Publishing, 1990.

Lucado, Max. *In the Grip of Grace*. Dallas: Word Publishing, 1996.

Morley, Patrick. *The Seven Seasons of a Man's Life*. Grand Rapids: Zondervan Publishing House, 1997.

Rediger, G. Lloyd. *Clergy Killers*. Louisville, Ky.: Westminster John Knox Press, 1997.

Spence, H.D.M. *The Pulpit Commentary*. Grand Rapids: W.M.B. Eerdmans Publishing Co., 1977.

Swindoll, Charles R. *Stress Fractures*. Portland, Ore.: Multnomah Press, 1990.

Tan, Paul Lee. *Encyclopedia of 7700 Illustrations*. Rockville, Md.: Assurance Publishers, 1979.

Thompson, J.A.K. *The Ethics of Aristotle*. New York: Allen & Unwin, 1953.

Tozer, A.W. *Root of the Righteous*. Harrisburg: Christian Publications, Inc., 1955.

Tzu, Sun. *The Art of War*, ed., James Clavell. New York: Bantam Doubleday Dell Publishing Group, Inc., 1983.

Vine's Complete Expository Dictionary of Old and New Testament Words. Nashville: Thomas Nelson, Inc., Publishers, 1985.

Webster's New World College Dictionary Fourth Edition. Foster City, Calif.: IDG Books Worldwide, Inc., 2001.

Zodhiates, Spiros. *The Complete Word Study Dictionary*. Chattanooga: AMG Publishers,1992.

Dr. Jeff Wickwire completed his undergraduate study at the University of North Texas. He continued his education at Luther Rice Seminary and Tyndale Theological Seminary, where he earned both his master's and doctoral degrees.

Jeff is known for his practical, clear and timely messages that "put something in your pocket you can carry home and use the next day." His vivid illustrations and common-sense approach to Scripture are widely known for making Christianity easy to understand and apply.

You can reach him at University Park Church, 1700 Rogers Rd., Fort Worth, TX 76107, or by e-mail at jlwick@upcfw.org.